B.C. PROVINCIAL POLICE STORIES

Dogs played an important role in helping to police the province. They were taken on strength as Constables and became one of the Force. (See page 138.) The above photo shows a police dog team on Tagish Lake in northwestern B.C. in April 1941. Constable C. N. Bennett the photographer-musher.

Design by John Moutray

Copyright © 1986, 1999 Heritage House Publishing Company Ltd.

Canadian Cataloguing in Publication Data

Clark, Cecil, 1899-
    B.C. Provincial Police stories

    ISBN 1-895811-77-5 (v. 1) — ISBN 1-895811-75-9 (v. 3)

    1. Criminals—British Columbia—History. 2. B.C. Provincial
Police—History. 3. Law enforcement—British Columbia—History. I. Title.
HV6809.B7C53 1999   364.1'09711   C99-910255-9

Printing History: First Edition - 1986
                    Reprinted - 1990, 1993
                    First Heritage House edition - 1999

Heritage House wishes to acknowledge Heritage Canada through the Book Publishing Industry Development Program, the British Columbia Arts Council, and the Canada Council for the Arts for supporting various aspects of our publishing program.

Front cover: The B.C. Provincial Police lock-up at Soda Creek was one of nearly 100 throughout the province that provided living quarters for a constable and cells for miscreants. At about $400 each, they were a bargain.

Photo credits: Cecil Clark 4, 6-7; Glenbow Archives 105; Heritage House 19, front and back covers; Public Archives of Canada 17 (C61937), 34-35 (16080); Bruce Ramsey 39; RCMP 104. All photos not otherwise credited are from the B.C. Provincial Archives.

HERITAGE HOUSE PUBLISHING COMPANY LTD.
Unit #8 – 17921 55th Ave., Surrey, B.C. V3S 6C4

Printed in Canada

CONTENTS

The B.C. Provincial Police's heritage goes back to 1858 gold rush to the Fraser River. During the subsequent Cariboo stampede their duties included being guards on the bullion-laden stagecoaches from Barkerville to Yale, above. They continued serving through the coming of the automobile, top right, to the jet age. In 1949 the Force received its first plane, bottom right, the famous de Havilland Beaver.

Foreword

When 17-year-old Cecil Clark joined the B.C. Provincial Police Force in 1916 it was then nearly 50 years old. It had the distinction of being not only the first police force in what is now Western Canada, but also Canada's oldest territorial force. When it was formed in 1858 there wasn't a mile of road on what is today the B.C. mainland, the Prairie was a lawless region known as Rupert's Land, while Canada was the name given to a small corridor along the St. Lawrence River to the Great Lakes. When the provinces of Alberta and Saskatchewan were created in 1905, the B.C. Police force was already nearly 50 years old, and in 1912 when Ontario and Quebec attained their present boundaries it had been upholding the law for 54 years.

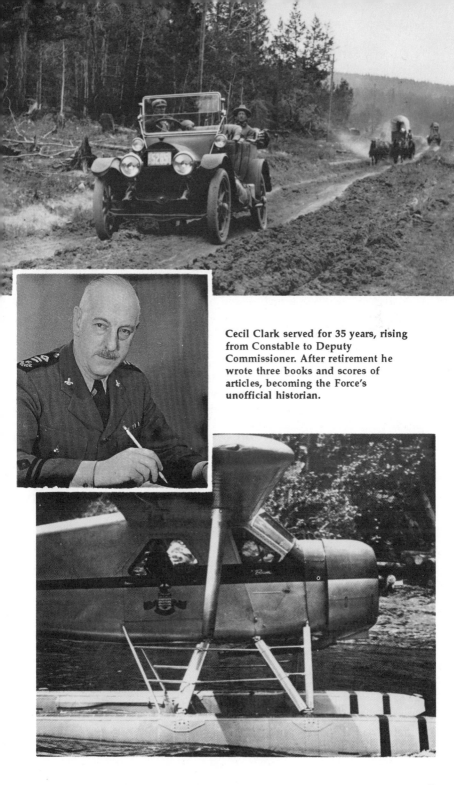

Cecil Clark served for 35 years, rising from Constable to Deputy Commissioner. After retirement he wrote three books and scores of articles, becoming the Force's unofficial historian.

When Cecil Clark joined the Force he little realized that he would serve for 35 years and, in a distinguished career, rise to Deputy Commissioner. One reason for his advancement was that he always displayed a deep interest in anything new. An avid motorcyclist, he suggested in 1920 that the Force needed a motorcycle highway patrol in view of the rapidly gaining popularity of the automobile. Later his idea became reality.

When the Force developed radiotelegraphy in the 1920s to combat massive communications problems that could see a letter take months for a round trip between Headquarters at Victoria and isolated Detachments, he learned Morse code to better understand this new development. Radiotelegraphy resulted in the Force establishing the first police communications network in North America.

When marksmanship training was instituted, Cecil was among the first to join. His score and that of others proved the need for such training. He got 93 out of a possible 300 points. A year later his score was almost perfect — 290 out of the possible 300 points, or 29 bulls eyes out of 30 shots. In addition, he became a regular contributor on firearms to *The American Rifleman,* North America's leading gun magazine.

On retirement in 1950, he became a full-time author and the Force's unofficial historian. He wrote scores of articles about the cases in which policemen were involved. The result was three books, two of which are still in print. (See Heritage House titles, *Stories of the B.C. Provincial Police—Volumes One and Two.* He also wrote several articles in this *Volume Three* and others in *Off Patrol: Memories of B.C. Provincial Policemen,* from which is taken much of the material in this Foreword.

What was it like when he joined the Force in 1916? On his first day at Headquarters a horse and buggy arrived, driven by Constable Macdonald of the Sidney Detachment. He had come 20 miles to deliver his monthly returns. In those days the police owned no transportation, although next year they were the proud possessor of two Model T Fords, one in Victoria and one in Vancouver. They had one telephone in the central office, with a sort of party line from it to the Superintendent's office.

The office routine at Victoria? Well, the letters, scores of them, were done on a typewriter. In the evening they were put into letter books which were volumes with thin rice paper in which were interleaved the letters with damp cloths. They were then put in a press, such being a contraption with a big lever which was screwed down. By this means the letters were imprinted on the thin rice paper. Pressure was exerted for five minutes, then the press was unscrewed. The letters, now being damp, were spread around to dry.

Since there was no filing system, the incoming letters were, in their volumes or binders, placed in a cabinet. If you wanted to see them and the answers you looked up an index, to and fro, from question to answer, from filing cabinet to letter book. It was a cumbersome arrangement, but they didn't know any better because there was nothing better. And such were the distances and transportation facilities that it could take four months or more for a policeman to get a reply to a letter.

During the almost century-long era that the B.C. Provincial Police were the front line of law and order they were always few in number. Even by 1900 there were only 100 to police an area larger than Washington, Oregon and California combined — with a sizeable chunk left over. Despite the awesome size of the region — as noted on page 118, a policeman being assigned to a Detachment could be several weeks just reaching it — they maintained the peace and well. Fourteen were killed doing so.

The first was Constable J. B. Ogilvie at Bella Coola in May 1865, the last was Constable Frank Clark at Victoria in November 1941.

For decades horses were the main means of travel in summer, with weeks in the saddle not uncommon. In winter, snowshoes and dog teams were used throughout the northern one-half of B.C. since there were virtually no roads. It wasn't unusual for a lone Constable on dog-team patrol to cover 400 and more miles and be out several weeks in the sub-zero cold and blizzards of northern B.C.

Other policemen were adept with rowboat and sailing sloop as they patrolled B.C.'s rocky, wave-washed coastline (See "The Rowboat Policemen" on page 130.) To police the stormy and foggy waters off the West Coast of Vancouver Island there were two Constables, Stanley Spain and James Seeley. These men were stationed at Clayoquot. To patrol their long and rugged coast line, they were furnished with a small sailing sloop, totally ineffective to cover the wild and rocky coast. In the 1890s came launches with open naphtha engines which were gradually replaced by a fleet of diesel-powered cruisers. Finally, arrived the air age and some officers piloted planes.

During their almost century-long service the far ranging officers readily embraced anything new that would make them more efficient. The first instance was in 1866. A gambler named John Barry was wanted for the murder of Charles Blessing between Quesnel and Barkerville. Constable John H. Sullivan of the nearby Richfield Detachment set out on horseback after him. He rode 100 miles to Soda Creek south of Quesnel but Barry had caught a stagecoach and was on his way to Yale. Fortunately, the Collins around-the-world telegraph line was under construction. The single wire had just reached Soda Creek but was not in commercial use since it was still being tested.

In 1858 Chartres Brew, above, was appointed the first Commanding Officer, thereafter all Commanders began their career as Constables.

Constable C. A. Prescott, opposite, was one of 14 officers killed on duty.

For the first 65 years, the officers were sent out with "a badge, a gun, handcuffs and billy club." Not until 1923 were uniforms adopted, below, beginning a series of improvements which made the B.C. Provincials one of North America's top police forces.

Constable Sullivan persuaded the operator to include a message to the Yale Detachment in his "test." As a consequence, Barry was arrested as he stepped off the stagecoach several days later. It was probably the first time in B.C. that a policeman used the telegraph to catch a criminal. John Barry was convicted and hanged at Richfield. (See Heritage House book, *B.C. Provincial Police Stories: Volume One.*)

But the officers were on duty not only when the telegraph arrived but also the telephone and electric light, and when the four-horse stagecoach gave way to the train, the automobile and the airplane. As already mentioned, they were proud that their experiments enabled them to establish the first city-to-city short wave police radio communication system in North America.

Whether assisting victims of fire or flood, escorting fugitives from foreign countries, or merely performing the daily routine of urban duty, these British Columbia policemen did it with pride born of a sense of history. The Force was especially proud that apart from the initial appointment of Chartres Brew, every man who rose to top command began his career as a Constable. Among them was John H. Sullivan who had used the new telegraph line to prevent murderer John Barry from escaping justice.

Early in the Force's history the policemen had gained the respect of the people they served. For instance, in 1864 at Wild Horse Creek in the East Kootenay an escaped convict called Charlie "One Ear" Brown murdered Constable Jack Lawson and fled to what he thought was safety across the border. But four miners felt otherwise. They tracked One Ear 40 miles into the U.S. and, as reported in the *British Columbian* newspaper: "Three of them raised their guns, double barrelled guns loaded with buckshot and fired simultaneously, literally riddling his dastardly body."

The Force's heritage dates to 1858 when gold was discovered on the Fraser River. That spring an influx of some 30,000 miners over the next few months changed the land forever. Until then what is today Mainland B.C. was controlled by the Hudson's Bay Company and generally known as New Caledonia. The only sign of white inhabitants were the Bay's fur trading posts linked by trails and supplied by brigades of pack horses. They included Fort Langley, Fort Kamloops, Fort George and Fort St. James.

Headquarters was on southern Vancouver Island at Fort Victoria, (today B.C.'s capital of Victoria). At the time Vancouver Island was a Crown Colony controlled by England, with James Douglas as Governor and a white population of about 800, some 300 at Fort Victoria. Into this quiet backwater of Empire stampeded the hopeful miners, most of them from California where the law was largely upheld by the six-gun and citizens' vigilante groups. For this reason the newcomers were virtually all armed. As one writer noted, each had "...the universal revolver, many of them carrying a brace of such, as well as a bowie knife."

Since there were no police to keep order, Governor James Douglas and British authorities were fearful that the incoming miners would clamor to have the region made part of the U.S. On July 7, 1858, Governor Douglas met the situation by appointing Augustus F. Pemberton as Commissioner of Police for Vancouver Island. Under Pemberton were a Superintendent, Chief Constable, Sergeant and five Constables. To control such a vast influx their numbers were pitifully few but they succeeded. That summer in Victoria the belt gun was banned which meant that the newcomers couldn't walk around carrying their beloved six-guns.

On the Mainland for several months of that hectic spring, summer and fall there wasn't even one lawman. To organize a constabulary, Britain's Colonial Secretary despatched 43-year-old Sub-Inspector Chartres Brew of the Royal Irish Constabulary. Immediately on Brew's arrival, Governor Douglas appointed him Chief Inspector of Police. The date was November 19, 1858, the swearing-in ceremony at Fort Langley on the Fraser River just east of today's Vancouver. At the same ceremony the Colony of British Columbia was born, with James Douglas becoming governor of both British Columbia and Vancouver Island.

At the end of 1859 the Colony was divided into six administrative districts. Overseeing each was a Magistrate who could hire six policemen of his choice and who had total power, including punishing offenders. A problem with the system was that there was no central control of the police — or the Magistrates. The solution was to appoint Chartres Brew the Gold Commissioner, effectively putting him in overall charge. In 1864 there was another move toward centralization when all appointments to the constabulary had to have the Governor's approval.

By then Brew's handful of locally recruited policemen had extended their activities to a new gold strike on Williams Creek in the Cariboo Country. Later they were on hand when a fresh bonanza was uncovered at Wild Horse Creek in the southeast corner of the Colony. Thereafter, whenever a miner found gold, a policeman was soon at his elbow.

Despite the fact that miners outnumbered policemen by hundreds — and even thousands — to one, there was remarkably little lawlessness. Hubert Howe Bancroft, the Pacific Northwest's foremost historian, observed: "Never in the pacification and settlement of any section of America have there been so few disturbances, so few crimes against life and property."

After nearly 12 years of faithful service in the Colony, Chartres Brew died on May 31, 1870, at Richfield in the Cariboo. He was buried in the cemetery at Barkerville and is commemorated by Mt.

Brew on the north side of beautiful Quesnel Lake in the Cariboo Mountains.

By then the Colonies of British Columbia and Vancouver Island had been united with police headquarters changed from New Westminster to Victoria. Then in 1871 there was another change. The Colonies became the Province of British Columbia, part of a new nation called Canada. Brew's Colonial police were now the B.C. Provincial Police. Two years later the North-West Mounted Police (today's RCMP) was formed and made the red serge the symbol of law and order on Canada's Central Plains. By then, however, their B.C. counterpart had been upholding justice west of the Rockies for 15 years.

As the province slowly grew — at Confederation its white population was only 9,000 — the Force expanded, but also slowly. In 1895, for instance, there were only 70 Constables scattered about the entire province, many doing very little police work. The bulk of their duties was collecting revenue, assessment of taxes and government agent's work in general. For instance, there was William Stephenson. He was stationed at Quesnelle Forks in the Cariboo. Besides being a Constable, he was also Mining Recorder, Collector of Revenue, and Justice of the Peace. He also acted as District Magistrate, and therefore could not do any actual police work.

Then there was Bill Parker at the 150 Mile House on the Cariboo Wagon Road. Bill patrolled the wagon road from Soda Creek to Bridge Creek during the summer months, nearly a 200-mile round trip. He was not paid during the winter, and had to provide his own horse and hotel expenses, as well as fodder and stabling for his horse. For all this he received during the summer $125 per month.

Another was Fred Wollaston, also stationed at the 150 Mile Post. He was a Special Constable on duty as a stagecoach guard. Millions of dollars in gold from the Barkerville area were sent by stage, and to discourage bandits, a police officer rode with the driver. He got $125 a month and had to furnish his own hotel accommodation and all personal expenses. Like Parker, he was paid only during the summer.

But not all Constables received such "high" wages. Fred Heal was a Special Constable at Victoria doing daily rural patrol work. He furnished his own horse and buggy and was paid $30 a month. In the Cariboo at Clinton, Constable George Mitchell also received $30 a month.

Accommodation for policemen ranged from basic to primitive. Many of them lived in the local lockup with their prisoners — everybody cosy in one room except that the prisoners had bars on their section. The one at Fort Steele in East Kootenay, for instance, like most was log, 33 feet long by 23 wide. It had the luxury of three rooms. The outer room was used by the police and also by the Public Works men who kept their tools in it. The inner room had three cells, and also was used as a kitchen. An adjoining room was used by Constable Barnes and his family. The logs were rotten and the wintry winds blew in through the chinks.

In addition, the Government was quite economical in those days. Bill Stephenson, Government Agent and Constable at Quesnelle Forks, thought a new lockup should be provided. Since a bridge was being taken down he had the sound timber brought up and used in the construction of the new quarters. The building cost $204.

But the one which Constable Jack Meek constructed at Mc-Dames Creek in the Cassiar in the 1930s was even more of a bargain. It cost a total of $20 for two windows — then Headquarters wouldn't pay for the windows because they "weren't necessary."

As already noted, the policemen were always few in number — incredibly few. For the first 40 or so years men in the field were very much on their own. They laid their own charges and prosecuted their own cases. There were even instances when they performed hangings.

On horseback in summer and snowshoes and dog teams in winter they travelled thousands of miles. The experience of Constable Robert Pyper who rode horseback over 400 miles in sub-zero Chilcotin weather to solve a murder is one example. (See page 32, "Constable Robert Pyper — Six Words to the Mile.")

In 1904 changing times were heralded by the introduction of the Motor Vehicle Act governing some 300 of the new automobiles then in the Province. Cost was $2 a car. In addition, the motorist had to pay for having a license plate made — a piece of leather to which was attached his number. To the police came the responsibility of maintaining records and enforcing the regulations, including conducting tests for driver's licences, the first in Canada.

But even into the 1930s conditions in some areas hadn't changed much, especially the Chilcotin and northern B.C. That was when Constable Stan Raybone and Game Warden Bill Broughten left Williams Lake for the Anahim Lake region on the track of two halfbreeds wanted for murder.

With a team and horses they left by sleigh on the first 200 miles. It took two weeks. Then they continued their search on snowshoes, knowing that the killers would shoot them on sight. They were unsuccessful, but in trying had travelled some 800 miles in winter conditions. In later years when Stan had retired as Inspector after 21 years in the Provincial Force and 14 in the RCMP, Cecil Clark asked him how the trip was.

"Pretty tough," he said. In fact that was all he said.

Policemen dressed for sub-zero cold at South Fort George in Central B.C. in 1912. To officers, B.C. presented a sea of mountains, a virtually roadless area where temperature could drop to -60°F and colder and for decades horses and dogs were the main transportation method.

The Force was nearly 30 years old before the first railway appeared, the C.P.R., shown below running down the main street of Kamloops in 1886. Prior to the railway, when the McLean gang (page 20) were transferred from Kamloops to New Westminster, the prisoners travelled by stagecoach, canoe, wagon and, finally, shuffled across the frozen Fraser River wearing 28-pound leg irons. The trip took seven days, a contrast to today's easy four-hour drive.

In his basement in 1928 Sergeant Carl Ledoux, above, built the Force's first portable shortwave radio equipment. Thereafter the Force built its own transmitter-receivers, so small that they could be used on dog-team patrols. As a result, the B.C. Provincial Police had the first police communications network in North America.

In 1935 Constable Jack Meek was sent to McDames Creek in the remote Cassiar area of Northwestern B.C. Just getting there took three weeks from Vancouver. He discovered that he had to police alone a virtually roadless area the size of England.

Winter duties included solitary dog-team patrols up to 500 miles long, a piece of canvas his only shelter in blizzards and temperatures of -40° F and colder. Just getting his mail involved a 500-mile return dog-team trip to Telegraph Creek on the Stikine River. (See the article, "One Man Detachment in Cassiar Country" in *Off Patrol: Memories of B.C. Provincial Policemen.*)

In addition to chasing law breakers, a task which befell Constables was searching for missing people. Fiercely independent trappers and prospectors in particular had problems when old age crept up and they refused to change their life style.

The experience of Constable H. O. Jamieson at Telegraph Creek in 1945 was a typical case. Hugh Ford, an old trapper who lived over 100 miles via wilderness trail from the nearest store, hadn't appeared on his annual supply trip and Constable Jamieson went to investigate. He was gone 15 days, travelling 410 miles, with 215 of them on foot carrying a pack through mountainous country. His feet did not heal for weeks. The old trapper had vanished but later the skeletons of his dogs were found.

Another case involved Constable J. C. Devlin. In the bitter cold of January 1934 he left Dawson Creek to bring in a trapper who had died a lonely death in his cabin which was 200 miles away. Constable Devlin and his companions were two weeks just reaching the cabin. The trek went into police records as "...merely a routine case and investigation."

Another instance of these outdoorsmens' independent attitude and the at times sad consequence was recorded at the Atlin Detachment in 1943. A watchman at the Tulsequah Mine reported that Jim MacGavin, an 82-year-old veteran prospector, had cremated himself in his log cabin.

The death was discovered when J. A. MacDonald, watchman at the Tulsequah Mine, found MacGavin's cabin burned to the ground. MacGavin, still physically strong and active despite his 82 years, lived alone in the cabin 12 miles from Tulsequah in northwestern British Columbia near the Alaska border.

MacDonald found a letter dated January 1943 in a bottle hanging by a string in MacGavin's woodshed. The letter said:

"Very ill with appendix trouble. This is the finish. Have no way to get to doctor and too weak to get wood. Hate to do it but best way seems to call it off and cremate outfit. — Jim."

In addition to remarkably few men policing an area so huge that the distance, as the crow flies, from Atlin Detachment in northwest B.C. via Vancouver to Sparwood in southeast B.C. is equivalent to travelling from Vancouver through the U.S. into Mexico, there was another handicap. The officers were dressed in civilian clothes. When they enlisted they were provided with a baton, handcuffs, gun and badge. That was it. No training. They had to learn on the job. These conditions remained essentially unchanged until 1923 when the Police and Prisons Regulations Act came into force. Thereafter the Force started on a program that was to make it one of the best — if not the best — law enforcement agencies in North America.

A khaki and green uniform was adopted, although the men had to pay for any alterations. They could wear oxfords instead of the issued boots — if they bought their own. In addition to introducing uniforms, the administrative structure changed. Out of the reorganization grew a system of policing municipalities under contract, a first for Canada. A Police Training School was started in Victoria in 1930 and a Criminal Investigation Branch established at Headquarters. Its specialists helped officers in the field to solve difficult crimes and it became part of a continent-wide clearing house for information on crimes and criminals.

Another first for North America was the use of radio which eventually gave all Detachments virtually instant contact with Headquarters. The police radio network was a homespun development. In 1928 Corporal Carl Ledoux demonstrated the practicability of shortwave radio on his home-made set. The demonstration was an immediate success and soon Ledoux had installations in Victoria, Vancouver, Nelson and Kamloops. Later the network was expanded to 22 stations, with other installations and operators on police boats.

The Force even developed portable radios. Carried like a small suitcase and weighing about 40 pounds, they could be used on dog-team patrols. The station took five minutes to assemble, each a complete sending and receiving unit which even included a pencil and message pad.

The radio was especially welcome to the Marine Division whose boats patrolled the province's 7,000 miles of coastline and were as isolated as any Northern outpost. The Division began very modestly with Constable A. D. Drummond patrolling the Gulf Islands in a rowboat. Then he was provided with a sail boat, the *Maybelle.* Since answering a call could take days if a contrary wind was blowing, the police heartily embraced the first motors, however cantankerous. Over the years the P.M.L. (Police Motor Launch) fleet grew until there were 14 boats from Vancouver to Prince Rupert.

Pride of the fleet was P.M.L. 14. She was 100 feet long and especially fitted to patrol Vancouver Island's West Coast, a treacherous area which has claimed some 250 vessels. Among them was the *Pacific* which sank on November 14, 1875, after a collision. Of over 250 passengers and crew, two survived. Among the dead was John H. Sullivan, who in 1866 had been the first policeman in Western Canada to use the telegraph to apprehend a murderer and had risen to command the Force. He was 42.

Since P.M.L. 14's ports of call included many isolated coastal communities, her facilities included five cells and the world's smallest courtroom — a virtual broom closet when compared with those ashore. The fact that P.M.L. 14 began her career as a rum runner didn't affect the quality of justice.

Another Division which found radios invaluable was the Highway Patrol, formed in 1935. Pavement was still in the future, the

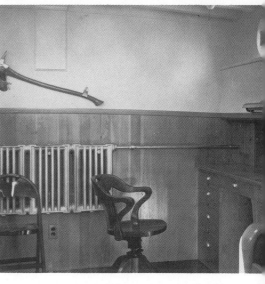

The Marine Division's 14 Police Motor Launches had the awesome responsibility of patrolling some 7,000 miles of coastline and scores of islands. The largest boat was P.M.L. 14, top, built in Halifax in 1927 as a rum runner at a cost of $77,000. In 1933 the police bought her for $23,000. During renovations one of her fuel tanks was removed and the space became a sea-going courtroom, above.

Center left: Icing during a hazardous trip to Prince Rupert.

Opposite: The crew of P.M.L. 8 whose beat was the stormy, rock-studded West Coast of Vancouver Island.

17

route of the "Highways" little changed from the original wagon and stagecoach roads of the province's frontier era. In 1929, for instance, Constable Bill Anderson was transferred to Nelson as one of the first motorcycle policemen. He picked up a new bike and sidecar in Vancouver and headed out. One dusty week later he reached Nelson.

But as the population grew and roads were improved, the Highway Patrol expanded until vehicles were travelling several million miles a year. To increase efficiency the Highway Patrol equipment was standardized, one of the first police forces in North America to do so.

Although horses, which for generations had been the main means of travel, were being used less and less, they still performed valuable service, with a Mounted Section formed in 1931. Stationed first in Victoria, it was later moved to Oakalla Prison Farm near Vancouver. The troop of horses provided escorts for distinguished guests and patrols for the more sparsely populated areas of the Lower Mainland. Many new recruits spent their first year or two with the Section, preparing themselves for Detachments in the Interior where horses were still a vital part of police work.

One government department which stemmed from the Provincial Police and with which the Force was closely affiliated for many years was the Game Branch. As noted in the booklet, *92 Years of Pride:*

"The game laws were indeed lax, for not long after the turn of the century a non-resident hunter was permitted for the fee of $50 to bag 10 deer, 3 caribou, 3 mountain sheep, 5 mountain goats, 2 moose and 2 elk! Also it was lawful to sell game in public markets. 'Shooting for the Market' caused ducks to be sold for 25 cents a pair, and there were cases such as 1,100 deer hides being sold to San Francisco, and a farmer at Princeton feeding his pigs on deer meat throughout the winter. Small wonder that there was growing demand to end such abuses, among them the serving of game in hotels and restaurants, on steamships and railway dining cars.

"In 1904 a special body was formed known as the Provincial Game Department, under much respected conservationist A. Bryan Williams. But a change in government in 1916 caused it to be replaced with the Game Conservation Board which was highly political and short-lived. Enforcement of game laws was again vested under the provincial police as the Game Branch, with Inspector Frank Butler in charge. In 1929 the Game Branch became a separate entity, a department of the provincial government, like the police directly responsible to the Attorney-General and later titled the Fish and Wildlife Service."

The last branch formed was the Air Division. On October 27, 1949, the Force received its first aircraft, a Beaver. The float plane, like the radio before it, greatly increased police effectiveness. Piloted by Sergeant Noel Beaumont, it was used for everything from mercy flights to regular police work. Its service, however, was brief. No, it didn't crash. In 1950 the Provincial Government for "reasons of economy" turned policing duties over to the RCMP under contract. Of the Force's 511 members, 482 became Mounties. The B.C. Provincial Police became history.

There is no official monument or other memorial to commemorate the service and sacrifice of these policemen. Even the Force's 92-year extensive collection of documents, thousands of photos and other historical records were virtually all destroyed by the RCMP when they took over. The reason is unknown. There is a small plaque, inconspicuous on a wall in a sunken garden, at the Provincial Museum-Archives building in Victoria. Erected by the B.C. Centennial Committee and the B.C. Provincial Police Veterans' Association, it states, in part:

"Formed on November 19, 1858, this, the oldest Territorial Police Force in Canada, served the people of British Columbia with honour, pride and unselfish duty until August 14, 1950.

"The 'B.C. Police' as it was commonly and respectfully known, demonstrated on land, sea and in the air, the highest qualities demanded of any Police Force in the world."

Nowhere is publicly displayed the names of the 14 officers who died on duty. To close this Introduction, they are:

Constable John D. B. Ogilvie, Bella Coola, May 1865
Constable John Lawson, Wildhorse Creek, April 1867
Constable John T. Ussher, Kamloops, December 1879
Special Constable Bob Williams, Little Fort, October 1907
Constable Geoffrey H. Aston, Okanagan Lake, March 1912
Constable Alexander Kindness, Clinton, May 1912
Constable Henry Westaway, Union Bay, March 1913
Constable George Stanfield, Grand Forks, June 1920
Constable Arthur W. Mable, Kamloops, September 1926
Constable Percival Carr, Merritt, May 1934
Inspector Wm. J. Service, Prince Rupert, July 1938
Sergeant Robert Gibson, Prince Rupert, July 1938
Constable Clifford A. Prescott, Princess Royal Island, June 1939
Constable Frank Clark, Victoria, November 1941

The Murdering McLean Gang

One of them was 15; two others, 17. They were, nevertheless, the most vicious outlaws ever to terrorize Interior B.C.

Deputy Commissioner Cecil Clark

In a little square of hallowed ground in Kamloops headstones identify the graves of pioneers who helped build British Columbia. One

Allan McLean.   Charlie McLean.

of them is the name John Tannatt Ussher and the words, "Departed this life Dec. 8th, 1879."

John Ussher was a Provincial Policeman, murdered on duty by four Kamloops outlaws who became known as the McLean gang.

The saga of this murderous group began with the father of three of them, Donald McLean. Born in Scotland in 1800, he grew into a strong, self-reliant, impetuous youth. He joined the Hudson's Bay Company when he was 20 and was assigned to the Bay's Western Region which included most of Western Canada and what is today Washington and Oregon. There was little of New Caledonia — later to become part of British Columbia — he was not familiar with. He commanded fur brigades, explored the wilder-

Archie McLean.   Alexander Hare.

ness, fought Indians and begot many sons by Indian wives.

There were two points in McLean's character that were outstanding — his impatience and his ungovernable temper. He had frequent altercations with his superiors and in his dealings with the Indians he was a ruthless bully.

Judge J. D. Swanson in his book, *Earliest Days in the Upper Country of B.C.*, cites the following incident:

"To avenge the killing by an Indian of one of the Company's servants — a young French-Canadian Cree half-breed of doubtful character — Alexis Belanger, Donald McLean and Montrose McGillivray at the head of 15 armed men were sent in January, 1849, by Donald Manson in search of Tlel, a young Indian, reported to have shot Belanger. Arriving at Quesnel they crossed the Fraser, and in a hut on the bank they found Tlel's uncle and his step-daughter and baby.

"'Where is Tlel?' cried out McLean, through his interpreter, Jean Marie Boucher.

"'Tlel is not here,' answered the uncle.'

"'Well, where is he? Answer me quick!'

"'How can I know,' replied the uncle. 'All I know is that he is not here.'

"'Then for today you shall be Tlel," declared McLean, who, firing with two pistols, missed but finally shot the innocent Indian dead with his musket. The son-in-law, hearing the shots, rushed in and was repeatedly shot till he fell lifeless. Thereupon his young wife, with a child in her arms, sought a place of refuge in the cabin, when a man from outside, probably by mistake, fired the contents of his musket, crushing the head of the baby, the ball lodging in the mother's shoulder.'"

Four years after these ruthless murders McLean was appointed Chief Trader at Fort Kamloops and then Factor at Fort Alexandria near present-day Quesnel. But in 1864 retribution was about to overtake this turbulent figure. The Chilcotin Indians had massacred 14 men out of 17 in a road-building gang and were on the war path. Whites in isolated settlements banded together for safety, and the Government took measures to bring the offenders to justice. McLean, who had incurred the lasting hatred of the Chilcotins, was singled out for special attention. Many an Indian lurked in the bush, his rifle waiting for McLean to come in view. That he seemed to bear a charmed life is more or less accounted for by the fact that he always wore an iron breast plate. On July 17, however, the Indians balanced the scales of justice. While McLean was on a scouting expedition looking for them he was shot in the back where he had no iron plate protection. His executioner, an Indian named Anukatlk, was never caught.

Subsequently, a number of Chilcotin Indians surrendered. For their participation in the Waddington massacre, five were hanged on the Fraser River bank at Quesnel. While all trace of their mass grave has disappeared, a link to the era is in Kamloops Museum. Here are Donald McLean's tobacco pipe and his sinister looking bowie knife, engraved with the words "Tower Hill, London."

So much for McLean the fur trader.

In 1879, McLean's second wife, Sophie, daughter of Chief Louis of the Kamloops band, lived near the community with her sons Allan, 25; Charles, 17; and Archie, 15. The first was a splendid physical specimen with jet black hair and beard, every inch a McLean. Charles took after his mother. He was tall and muscular, but with beetling brows and — as contemporary reports had it — "a glance that at times was anything but frank and pleasant." Archie, the youngest, was fairly tall for his age, with dark hair and eyes and a swarthy skin. Nearby lived a stepbrother, Hector McLean.

Accustomed to a wild frontier life from birth, the McLean boys lived in the saddle. They could ride as soon as they could walk, rope anything moving or still, and were excellent shots with a rifle or pistol. They spoke the French-Indian patois, as well as the common Indian Chinook and English.

Toward the fall of 1879, settlers in the Nicola-Okanagan districts began to talk of the McLeans. They had formed a gang which included Alex Hare, the 17-year-old French half-breed son of a rancher named Nick Hare.

One of the McLeans got into a fight with an Indian and bit off his nose. He served a few months in jail for this offence and came out with a thirst for vengeance. Property, particularly livestock, was not safe when the McLeans were around. A Chinese was robbed by the gang and so badly beaten over the head by a gun butt that he nearly died. These wild actions were accompanied by wilder talk. The McLeans always threatened their victims with violence. Tragically, they were not jesting.

The Provincial Constable at Kamloops was John Ussher. He was 35, son of a clergyman and had been married about 18 months. "Johnny" Ussher, as the townspeople called him, was respected by the community. He was well known to the McLeans, having arrested them for minor offences from time to time.

One day early in December 1879, rancher William Palmer who lived about 35 miles from Kamloops reported that his black horse had been stolen. Palmer had seen Charles McLean in possession of the animal. With him were his brothers, Allan and Archie, and Alex Hare. He told Ussher that he had ridden up to the four men and recognized one of them astride his black horse. As he approached, he heard the ominous click of weapons being cocked.

"Don't shoot," said Palmer, "I'm not after you."

"You hadn't better," said Allan McLean quietly. The boys told Palmer of some trouble they had with a rancher named Moore and spoke of "bringing him to time" and, said Archie, "We'll kill any bastard who comes to arrest us."

On the basis of Palmer's statement, a warrant was issued for the arrest of the McLeans. Knowing that the boys acted as a gang, Constable Ussher first arrested their stepbrother, Hector. Then the officer swore in Palmer and another man named Shumway as Special Constables.

As they took the trail on December 7, Ussher told his companions that he didn't think there would be any trouble in arresting the gang. Just after dark they reached John McLeod's Ranch. He agreed to join them next morning at a place called Government Camp. Soon it was apparent that they were on the right track, for at one spot in the freshly fallen snow hoof marks led deeper into a thick patch of bush. Suddenly, in a clearing they saw four saddled horses.

"They'll never fire a shot," said Ussher. "Come on, I'll take the lead."

They had ridden but a few paces when Charlie McLean was noticed half hidden behind a tree, his rifle showing. The posse reined up.

"I don't see my black horse," said Palmer.

Charlie McLean gave a sharp whistle. A shot rang out and the bullet cut through Palmer's ice-coated beard. "That was a close one," he said, trying to control his startled horse. But the same ball had hit John McLeod. He dismounted, blood spurting from his cheeks.

Then Allan McLean fired from behind the tree. Palmer, armed with a shotgun, tried to get a shot at him as he dodged behind another tree. Allan fired again.

Ussher's horse, startled by the shooting, plunged and reared. Ussher slipped from the saddle. A less courageous man might have been tempted to take cover, but Ussher knew his duty. He had a revolver in his saddle holster but left it there, perhaps thinking that his previous contact with the McLeans had earned their respect. It was a tragic misjudgment.

Ussher called on them to surrender. Then, amid the deadly fusillade, walked towards Alex Hare. Hare advanced, hunting knife in one hand, revolver in the other. The Constable grasped the young man by the shoulder. They grappled. Hare struck repeatedly with the knife. Down went Ussher, Hare astride him, Again and again Hare used the knife, slashing Ussher in the face.

Allan McLean was heard to shout, "Kill the...."

Fifteen-year-old Archie darted from the shelter of a tree, revolver in hand. Holding it close to Ussher's head, he fired. Ussher lay still.

Donald McLean, above, father of the McLean boys, and John McLeod, wounded in both cheeks by a bullet which passed through William Palmer's beard.

John McLeod, although hampered by the wound to his face, blasted at the outlaws with his shotgun until he was shot in the leg. As Allan McLean was loading his gun, Palmer rode in and fired at him but missed. Shumway was unarmed and could only take cover. After exchanging about 30 shots, the beaten posse rode back to Kamloops for help.

The townspeople were horrified to hear of the fate of Constable Ussher. Horses, arms and ammunition were hastily collected and a large body of horsemen galloped out of town to catch up with the McLeans. Arriving at the outlaw's camp just after dark, they found the camp fire still burning. Ussher's body was frozen stiff. The outlaws had stripped off his coat, boots and gloves.

In the meantime, the McLeans had ridden up to Tom Trapp's homestead some seven miles away. Trapp recognized them. "What do you fellows want?" he asked.

Charlie and Archie cocked their weapons and said they wanted firearms and ammunition. Eyeing the weapons, Trapp told them to go into the house and take what they wanted. As Allan McLean and Hare dismounted, Trapp noticed a pair of handcuffs dangling from Allan's hand. He also noticed they were bloodstained. Apprehensively, he studied the others.

"You've got blood on you," he said to one of them.

"Yes, Ussher's blood. We killed him." Charlie brandished a knife and boasted of the murder, threatening to kill anyone who came after him. Hare and Allan, in fact, debated whether they should shoot Trapp. But they appeared to have had second thoughts and rode away with Trapp yelling after them, "You'd better surrender or leave the country."

In the evening they stopped at another homestead where a man named Roberts was killing a pig. He looked up to see four young horsemen around him and noticed they swung their rifles down. "Good evening," he said civilly. "It's a cold night."

"It sure is," answered Charlie, "and a hell of a lot of colder nights coming."

To which the youngest one added, "and a damn sight hotter times, too."

Allan and Archie dismounted and approached Robert's fire, pulling revolvers as they asked for a man named Johnson. Apparently they had some score to settle with him.

"He's on his own place," said Roberts.

Then they asked about Canada, a local Indian noted for his bravery and who was credited with once tangling with three bears. The gang mentioned this incident and Allan said, "This'll be the last night he'll have to face three bears."

"He'll have to face four boys," Archie added. "I'm only 15 but you bet your life I'm brave."

They then told Roberts they had killed Constable Ussher. "You're fooling," Roberts replied, unbelievingly.

"You bet we killed him," said Allan.

"Here's the knife that went through him, and here's his blood on it," said Hare.

Archie held up one foot, "Here's his boots."

"And here's his coat and gloves," added Hare.

Roberts was horrified, but the McLeans had not finished. "There's his horse, saddle and canteen," said Allan. Then he went on to describe how William Palmer had ridden in and tried to shoot him. He pointed to some holes in his coat and boastfully hauled Ussher's handcuffs from the saddle bag.

"Here's the handcuffs that Ussher brought to put on me — but he didn't get them on. I'll keep them for Palmer."

"Yes," broke in Charlie, "and we'll give him 50 lashes every day and 50 every night before he goes to bed." At this, Allan and Charlie laughed heartily.

They mentioned two ranchers named Ben and Sam Moore and boasted they were going to "get" them. Sickened by this talk, Roberts remarked, "I don't give a damn what you do. You can kill me if you want to."

"No, we don't want to kill you," Allan replied. "You've a large family."

And with that the boys rode off. Next day, near Stump Lake, they spied a man named Kelly who worked as a shepherd for a settler. Kelly was sitting on a high rock.

"I'll bet I could bring him down from here," bragged Charlie McLean.

There was one report from his rifle and the unfortunate Kelly slithered down the rock, dead. Hare ran forward and took a watch and chain from the body.

On they went, boasting of their exploits to workers at Thomas Scott's Ranch. Farther south at William Palmer's Ranch they forced Palmer's wife to hand over firearms and ammunition, threatening to kill anyone who barred their path.

The gang slept that night at an Indian rancherie at the head of the Nicola River. Seeking sanctuary with the Indians was part of Allan's plan and the reason for collecting all the arms and ammunition they could find. If a posse pursued them the gang would arm the Indians and precipitate an uprising. It would spread like bushfire, and the scattered settlements would have something more important to think about than the immediate capture of the McLeans. In any event, even if only a few Indians joined, the whole Nicola Valley would for the time being be at their mercy as the settlers were widely scattered and lacked arms.

Next morning the gang rode in to an Indian ranch at the foot of Douglas Lake. They stabled their horses and stayed that day and night.

In the meantime, the posse from Kamloops increased in numbers and the telegraph wire to Victoria hummed. The Superintendent of Police hastened by schooner to Port Angeles, Washington, to alert U.S. authorities to watch the border crossing. B.C. lawmen, however, did not think the McLeans would cross the line for they had fought with American Indians and usually worsted them. On one occasion the gang had stolen some horses and an Indian woman and shaved her head. This was the ultimate insult, assuring the McLeans a deadly reception from Washington braves.

The Kamloops posse, led by Justice of the Peace John Clapperton, had by now learned of the outlaws' whereabouts and converged on the cabin they occupied. They were told that a man named Thomas Richardson had parleyed with the gang through two Indians friendly to them. Richardson told the outlaws that they should surrender.

"Never," they yelled, "death before surrender."

When Clapperton heard this news he decided that no unauthorized person should meet with the outlaws. If the Indians were disposed to be friendly to the besieged boys, a general fight might ensue. Clapperton sent word to Chief Shillitnetza to stop all communication between his people and the McLeans. The Chief cooperated fully, telling the whites "to shoot any Indian going or coming from the McLean cabin."

Clapperton knew that they had neither food nor water and must eventually give up or commit suicide. He split the posse into three shifts so that there was a constant watch. "Shillitnetza" was the password.

Morning came with no sign of life from the small cabin, though later in the day Clapperton detected through field glasses signs that thirst was troubling the boys. They had torn up the cabin's floor to reinforce the walls, and through a chink in the logs could be seen attempting to scrape in a little snow. Rifle bullets from the posse smashing into the logs quickly stopped the attempt. Then they tried poking straws through to suck up any moisture. Apart from this activity, the day passed uneventfully. On December 11, a second party of settlers arrived under the leadership of another J.P. named Edwards.

Then Clapperton asked Chief Shillitnetza if his son, Saliesta, would take a message to the McLeans under cover of a white flag. The Indian boy agreed and Clapperton wrote out the following message:

McLean Bros. and Alex Hare: Will you surrender quietly? If so, send in your arms and I guarantee your personal safety. No surrender, and we burn the house over your heads.

Jn. Clapperton, J.P.

With the Indian messenger paper and pencil were sent for a reply. Saliesta reined his horse about 300 feet from the cabin and waved his signal of truce. Finally, through a crack in the cabin door a tiny piece of rag fluttered for a moment in the raw December air. The Indian moved to within speaking distance. More minutes passed. He advanced to the door and was handed a paper. Bending low in the saddle, Saliesta galloped back to the watching ranchers.

On the scrap of paper, Clapperton read:

"Mr. Clapperton,
Sir:—
The boys say that they will not surrender, and so you can burn the house a thousand times over.

Alexr. J. Hare.
I wish to know what you all have against me. If you have anything, please let me know what it is.

A.H.

Clapperton decided to carry out his threat and burn the cabin. Large bundles of hay were dragged into position and saturated with coal oil, but they were wet and refused to burn. For two hours they tried — two hours fraught with danger for the McLeans kept up a desultory fire all the time. In his report on the siege Clapperton noted: "The bullets shot at the bales passed through with deadly force so that the breastwork was useless."

Clapperton decided to try another parley. A posse member, John Leimard, offered to carry the flag. When the gang agreed to a truce, Clapperton learned that hunger and thirst were doing their work, that the boys were in bad shape. He returned to the cabin with pencil and paper and the outlaws laboriously wrote:

We will surrender if not ironed and supplied with horses to go to Kamloops.

A message was sent back:

Surrender by coming outside and laying down your arms. We will protect you.

Grim-faced ranchers with cocked rifles carefully watched the little log structure. Then the door slowly opened and one by one the outlaws appeared. They discharged their firearms in the air, then threw them on the ground. By this act they showed their Indian ancestry. It was common practice when Indians surrendered to fire off unused ammunition.

Tired and drawn, their tongues swollen from thirst, the McLean gang staggered forward. Their six revolvers, five rifles and two shotguns were gathered up, they were handcuffed and placed in a wagon for Kamloops. In the cabin, searchers found John Kelly's watch and chain.

The gang had been captured with only one casualty. A man whose horse had strayed too near the cabin was shot in the chest when he tried to retrieve the animal. Fortunately, it was only a flesh wound.

At Kamloops the four were committed for trial on charges of murder. Hare made a partial confession, and intimated that the gang had expected aid from the Nicola Indians.

The prisoners were taken to New Westminster via Cache Creek and the Cariboo Wagon Road to Yale, Constables Shuler, Crotty and Burr their escort. From Yale, the first 30 miles was by two canoes, the prisoners lying shackled in the bottom. Then ice in the Fraser River obstructed any further progress. At Cheam the escort procured a wagon and made the rest of the journey by road. The Fraser River was frozen over to a point above Harrison River, and the Constables with their heavily shackled prisoners crossed the ice on foot at New Westminster. The prisoners were locked up at 11:00 o'clock on Christmas Day, 1879. The trip had taken seven days.

At New Westminster a special Assize opened on March 13, 1880, at which the McLeans and Hare faced the bar of justice. Hector McLean, the oldest brother, charged with aiding and abetting, was held in jail to be dealt with later.

At the end of the trial, Mr. Justice Crease charged the jury in a two-hour speech remarkable for its clarity and force. He complimented the settlers of the Kamloops area for their adherence to the principles of British justice, implying that on other soil the McLeans would probably have been lynched.

The jury took 22 minutes to find them guilty. Justice Crease then sentenced them to death. On hearing the sentence, Hare remarked, "It's a well deserved sentence, your Lordship."

The prisoners shambled out of court in their unwieldy leg irons. When Allan passed William Palmer he viciously kicked him in the leg. The Constable in charge struck Allan with a cane and Archie lashed out at him before being hustled to the cells. They continued to be troublesome prisoners and there were repeated attempts at escape, in addition to bursts of disorderly conduct.

The McLeans appealed their sentence on the legal grounds that as no commission had been issued, there was no Assize, and therefore no trial. The Supreme Court of British Columbia agreed with them, and on June 27, 1880, ruled that the prisoners had been illegally tried. They were to remain in custody until discharged by due course of law.

At Kamloops in October, Hector McLean was acquitted of being an accessory before the fact. A month later, Allan, Charles and Archie McLean, with their accomplice, Hare, were once more placed on trial in New Westminster for the murder of Ussher and Kelly.

Again, the jury found them guilty. The second trial had only served to delay their execution. In confinement they became more unruly than ever and had to be chained to the walls of their cells for days at a time. On one occasion Archie threatened the Warden with an iron bucket, on another a knife was found in Allan's blankets. On one routine examination, prison officers discovered that his irons were partially filed through with a file suspected to be from another prisoner.

Then one day a prisoner, John Henry Makai, asked the Warden if he could act as executioner for the McLeans. Puzzled by this odd request, the Warden told Makai that an official executioner would be used. However, he kept Makai under observation and later learned that the McLean gang had made a compact with him. If Makai was appointed executioner he would secretly cut through the execution ropes and when the trap was sprung, the outlaws would drop unharmed. They would then whip out knives and cut their way to freedom. Makai, on release, was to be rewarded with 100 head of cattle and 40 horses, which he would collect from brother Hector in Kamloops.

For the McLeans, however, there would be no escape. On January 28, 1881, the *New Westminster Mainland Guardian* reported:

"A SINISTER DISPLAY - As we passed the gate of our city gaol yesterday morning, we observed the pieces of timber all cut and shaped in readiness to put together to form the scaffold on which the McLeans and Hare are to suffer death on Monday morning next. It is bad enough that their minds are now dwelling on their approaching end, but to have their ears assailed with the tap, tap, tap of the hammers that nail together the 'fatal gallows tree' is something terrible to endure...."

The hanging went as scheduled on January 31, the paper reporting: "Monday morning dawned cold, sharp, and clear. At 7:30 quite a group of our leading citizens had gathered within the four walls of the city prison....

"The condemned men were early attended by their spiritual advisors, Revd. Father Horris and two other priests.... A little before 8 a.m., the executioner proceeded to pinion them by means of stout leather straps: the hands were fastened in front, and a strap passing above the elbows behind....

"...The Hangman then adjusted the ropes, commencing with Hare; the signal was given by the Sheriff, then in an instant the doomed men fell. Death appeared to have been almost instantaneous; with the exception of Charlie, who showed slight convulsions, they scarely moved a muscle. After hanging the usual time, the bodies were cut down and decently interred. After the drop fell, something like a sigh of relief escaped from the spectators, who felt that innocent blood had been avenged, and the law vindicated."

But the story of the McLean boys did not end here.

Four years later in 1885, Alexander McLean, eldest of two sons of old Donald McLean's first wife, ran amok on the Indian Reserve at Kamloops. He killed one man and wounded four others. Chief Louis and his braves, clad in full war panoply, surrounded and killed him.

His death was the end of the McLean's lawless era. A son of ill-fated Allan McLean, for instance, served in France during World War One with the Canadian Army. At Vimy Ridge in April 1917 he attacked a German dugout, killing 19 of the enemy and capturing 21. He won the Distinguished Conduct Medal, although his comrades said he should have been awarded the Victoria Cross, the nation's highest award for bravery.

The official reports from the officers who policed
B.C. were often marvels of brevity. Take, for
instance, those of

Constable Robert Pyper — Six Words to the Mile

by Deputy Commissioner Cecil Clark

Throughout the almost century long era from 1858 to 1952 that B.C.
Provincial Police maintained law and order they were spread thin.

Very thin, in fact. In the early 1900s
there were only 100 Provincials for
the entire province, fewer than Vancouver's police force.

One major reason the few Provincials were able to effectively
police their vast domain was that
residents were fundamentally more
law abiding than today and readily
assisted whenever necessary. In
1898, for instance, no one was
charged with assaulting or obstruct-
ing a police officer. One of the main
problems was the swinging doors of
the saloons which were a feature of
frontier life. In 1898, 33 per cent of
arrests were for being drunk and
disorderly.

Another advantage that pioneer
policemen had over their modern
counterparts was a minimum of
paper work, a contrast to today's

Constable Robert Pyper at the Soda Creek
lockup in the early 1900s. Nearly 100
lockups were built throughout the
Province. The Soda Creek one still stands,
top right, and should be preserved.

mountains of official reports, forms and other time-consuming red tape. For many years the major paperwork confronting the provincials was the Daily Provincial Police Reports. These were two-page forms which allowed three lines for each day. At month's end these reports were submitted to the District Chief who then sent them to Victoria. Although the Daily Reports vanished in the early 1920s, some still survive in the Provincial Archives in Victoria.

Among them are some submitted in 1898 by Provincial Police Constable Robert Pyper who was in charge of the newly opened Alexis Creek Detachment in the Chilcotin, west of Williams Lake. They embodied a brevity in sharp contrast to modern practice.

Take, for instance, June 5 when he rode 44 miles to Riske Creek and on the 6th "...arrested Michell, an Indian, for horse stealing." Seven words, good for a thousand today.

Then, with his prisoner, he rode 28 miles to Hanceville where, he reports, "Prisoner escaped. In pursuit."

The remaining two lines for that day are blank. The reason became evident in his report for the next day which notes: "Recaptured prisoner at Puncheon Creek, 50 miles from Hanceville. Left Puncheon creek, arrived Alexis Creek...."

In that report he used 17 words. It was totally extravagant, virtually a book by Pyper's standards. All he had done was ride over 100 miles on horseback, recapture his prisoner single-handed, then bring him back to the local lockup — six miles to the word.

According to old-timers who knew Pyper, he always rode a white stallion. This particular June he covered 523 miles in the saddle. He was one of the better paid Constables for he got $100 a month plus $25 for the upkeep of his horse. The horse money was a bit of a bonus. In summer there was always a convenient hay meadow, and wherever he stopped overnight, people were glad to see him and fed his horse.

Here's another example of his laconic style:

"July 13th - Soda Creek to 150 mile ... 28 miles.

"14th - at 150 mile

"15th - 150 Mile to Alkali Lake. Arrested Louis Spahn, Indian for attempted murder.

"16th - Alkali Lake to 150 Mile ... 38 miles

"17th - 150 Mile to 111 Mile (39 miles)

"18th - 111 Mile to 59 Mile (52 miles)

"19th - 59 Mile to Ashcroft. Handed prisoner over to Chief Constable Burr for Escort to Kamloops gaol."

Next day he started back to Alexis Creek, some 140 miles up the Cariboo Wagon Road with its stagecoaches and ox-drawn freight wagons to 150 Mile House, then 75 miles westward through the sparsely populated Chilcotin to Alexis Creek. His total journey was easily 500 miles, yet delivering his prisoner to Chief Constable

Burr at Ashcroft took only five brief lines in his Daily Report. In contrast with today, when he arrived at Ashcroft there were no flashing lights, no radio reporters with out-thrust microphones, no glaring TV cameras, no newspaper reporters. A simple 12-word statement: "Handed prisoner over to Chief Constable Burr for Escort to Kamloops gaol."

Pyper did not even consider the details of the murder important. His duty was to arrest the suspect and deliver him some 150 miles. He successfully concluded his task in 5 days — and five entries in his Daily Provincial Police Report.

Pyper was born in Nanaimo and served with the B.C. Police at Rossland before being transferred to Alexis Creek in 1897. That Christmas he had a murder to investigate. A 17-year-old Chilcotin Indian called Samien shot and killed Lewis Elkins, a young Englishman running a store at Quetsin Lake, about 12 miles southwest of Tatla Lake.

After the murder, Samien took the storekeeper's keys and fitted himself with a new shirt, coat, pants and boots. Then he headed for Nemiah Valley on Elkins' horse. Somewhere along the trail he stole two fresh mounts to cover 60 miles in 14 hours. Young Samien, however, couldn't resist boasting about his exploit. Soon word reached the dead man's brother, Ed, at Chilko Lake.

Ed saddled up and reached the murder scene on New Year's Eve. His brother's body was slumped over a pine table in the kitchen, a bullet in the back of his head. Elkins then rode 85 miles to Alexis Creek to tell Pyper, who promptly set off to investigate. Afterward the policeman rode east and south 120 miles until he caught up with his quarry. He held a preliminary hearing before Justice of the Peace Franklin, then escorted his prisoner over 150 miles to 150 Mile House, the temperature -20°F and a foot of snow on the ground.

At 150 Mile House another Constable took Samien by stagecoach to Ashcroft, where still another Constable escorted him on the eastbound train to Kamloops jail. On the way Samien tried to escape but didn't make it. He ended with a life sentence. By the time Pyper got back to his Detachment, he had covered close to 250 miles in the saddle.

Pyper, after eight years with the Provincial Police, went into the fur trade at Chilanko Forks in the Chilcotin. At this outpost he handled about $25,000 worth of fur a year under the name of Williams Lake Trading Company. He continued in business through the 1930s, moving into a new building which one night mysteriously burned to the ground.

Provincial Police Sergeant Frank Gallagher came from Williams Lake to investigate. He soon dismissed the idea that Pyper had caused his own fire, but being a bit baffled, rode over to Redstone

Reserve and had a chat with the chief. The result was that he got the assistance of two young Indians, Teddy and "Doc" English.

At the charred ruins of the building, Gallagher's sharp-eyed assistants found the tracks of two men. White men, they said. Indians walk in a different way. They noted also that one man had a patch on his moccasin. Then about a mile away Doc English found the remains of a fire. "White man's fire," he observed. "Indian don't use paper to start fire."

Then Doc was absent for a day and returned with additional news — he had found two white men in a cabin. He had traced the patched moccasin without being seen. Although the cabin was 20 miles away, Sergeant Gallagher didn't doubt him. He proceeded to the cabin, although in a vehicle. The gasoline era was replacing the horses of Constable Pyper's days, but since the "road" permitted a speed of only 15 miles an hour, the improvement was not exactly spectacular.

The cabin was a sort of soddy, the rear dug into a bank. Inside were two trappers who gave their names as Purkett and Rudland. The latter was wearing the patched moccasin. Gallagher took him in charge. On the way back, Rudland said he didn't see why he should be charged and Purkett left in the clear. It seems that Purkett had a grudge against Pyper and counselled the crime. Rudland said he got a can of coal-oil, broke into the store at night, and set it on fire. Back at the scene he showed Gallagher the empty coal-oil can he had tossed in the bush.

Later Rudland was sentenced to three years for arson and Purkett five for conspiracy. Sergeant Gallagher, who functioned in a more modern age, had to belt out a few 2,000-word reports!

Although Bob Pyper started to rebuild his store, it unfortunately never got higher than the walls. He was now 70, and suffered from throat cancer. Despite the fact that his nearest neighbors were 14 miles to the east and 30 miles to the west, he refused to leave. Because of the isolation the only traffic for certain was a once-weekly mail service operated by T. H. Hodgson.

In March, Jack Hodgson stopped at Pyper's cabin beside the partly completed store. There was no sign of activity, with the cabin door fastened on the inside. Jack managed to get in through a window and found Pyper dead in bed, his body frozen solid.

He was buried near Alexis Creek and is commemorated by Pyper Lake.

The murdered trapline partners. Hans Pfeuffer, top left, was shot in the leg then the killer watched him freeze to death. Eugene Mesmer, bottom left, with a marauding black bear, was shot twice in the back.

Alex Prince, above right, the nomad who turned murderer.

The cold northern moon shone on the frozen bodies of the two trappers, one of them guarded by his Newfoundland dog. For them

Death Came On Moccasined Feet

by Deputy Commissioner Cecil Clark

Early in 1944 some 30 miles north of the junction of the Finlay and the Parsnip Rivers in Northern B.C. stood the trapping cabin of Eugene Mesmer and Hans Pfeuffer. Known as "the German boys," Mesmer, 35, was a one-time upholsterer turned trapper, and 42-year-old Pfeuffer had served in the German army. With the rise of Hitler the pair left Germany and by 1944 had been trapping on the

Finlay River about seven years. They were well known and well liked by everyone, and river travellers were always sure of a hospitable welcome at what became known as Mesmer's Landing. Both were keen amateur photographers, and Mesmer's skill as an upholsterer and cabinet maker made their cabin almost a show place. It was March, the lonely wilderness still locked in the icy grip of winter. Three men, trudging on snowshoes down the frozen river, looked forward to the warmth and comfort of Mesmer's cabin if they could reach it before dark. One was Jack Maguire, another a storekeeper called Ben Corke, and the third was Hudson's Bay Company employee John Ware, grandson of Fort Ware's founder. They had already snowshoed some 30 miles dragging a sled of fur and had another 30 or so to go before reaching Finlay Forks where they were heading for the annual fur auction.

In the waning light Ware suddenly saw something dark on the ice ahead. When the trio reached it they found a man, face down on the ice, snowshoes on his feet. Not only was he frozen stiff but frozen to the ice, meaning they couldn't turn him over to make identification. After a brief discussion the travellers wheeled about and headed back to Fort Grahame, some 27 miles upstream. There, with the Hudson's Bay Company's small portable transmitter, they flashed word of death in the wilderness to B.C. Provincial Police District Sergeant George H. Clark at Prince George, some 200 miles to the south. He and his 15 men were the law in a sprawling wilderness of some 44,000 square miles, a virtually roadless area three times larger than Holland.

Following the wireless message, however, came a complication for Sergeant Clark. Just after Maguire, Corke and Ware had left their tragic find, a prospector named Don Gilliland, travelling alone upriver from the Forks, rounded a bend in the river near Mesmer's Landing. He, too, saw something dark on the ice. But this object was moving. Unslinging his rifle when he got closer, he saw it was a big black Newfoundland dog — Pfeuffer's dog, Rex. When he saw the stranger, the dog headed over to the river bank and crouched on the ice beside a man who lay prone. Gilliland saw it was Pfeuffer, lying dead on his side in a pool of frozen blood. Gilliland, aghast at the sight, tried to move the body but Pfeuffer was frozen to the ice. Gilliland camped nearby for the night, and at daylight started the 27-mile trek back to Finlay Forks to advise Prince George by radio.

With two reports of dead men on the Finlay, George Clark concluded that two parties had seen the same dead man.

He promptly despatched Constable H. L. (Harry) McKenney to the scene in a ski-equipped Fairchild piloted by veteran bush pilot Pat Carey. The plane picked up Gilliland at Finlay Forks then they flew downriver to Pleuffer's body. They landed on the Finlay River below the trapper's silent cabin and Constable McKenney walked upstream to Pfeuffer's body. He was astonished to find near it a large cavity melted into the ice. From dog hairs it was obvious that Rex had for several days maintained a futile vigil beside his dead master. When they left, the men took the loyal dog with them.

At the scene, McKenney followed bloodstains on the ice to note where Pfeuffer had rested, then further on the place where he had first fallen when felled by an assailant's bullet. He put the body aboard the plane and flew back to Finlay Forks. Then he picked up Jack Maguire who guided him to the second body, just around the bend of the river from where Pfeuffer fell. The second dead man was discovered to be Mesmer, who had also been shot.

McKenney then turned his attention to the partners' cabin. Though it was locked, the key was in Mesmer's mackinaw pocket. The cabin was about 20 by 30 feet, with beds at opposite corners, a table in the middle, at one side a stove and the usual cupboards and shelving. In one corner stood a console model battery-operated radio. A rug on the floor and overstuffed chairs made the place quite comfortable

McKenney checked for firearms but found none. Then he thought of the dead men's photographic skill and looked for cameras. There were none. Then the policeman walked around outside, looking for strange tracks, finally ascending the ladder to the Germans' food and fur cache.

It was near the cabin, raised about 10 feet above ground, the posts wrapped with tin to deter wandering rodents. McKenney's experienced eye noted the food was ample, though there was something queer about the fur catch. There were lots of wolf, lynx and coyote pelts but, strangely enough, no small furs. The valuable ones — mink, marten and weasel were missing.

Back by plane to the Forks, Constable McKenney paused long enough to drop Maguire. Then with the two bodies flew back to Prince George. There, it took some time before the bodies thawed out to permit medical examination. Finally the police learned that Pfeuffer had been hit in the back of the right thigh, the bullet fracturing his femur. After being wounded, said the doctor, Pfeuffer died of exposure. Mesmer had been shot twice in the back. One of the bullets was recovered and sent to the B.C. Police Criminal Investigation Department at Victoria for ballistic study.

This done, Sergeant Clark set off for the scene of the killing with McKenney and Game Warden Alf Jank. The latter would be particularly valuable for he had been stationed at Finlay Forks for two years and knew everyone in the area.

It was Jank who voiced the suspicion that a young 23-year-old Indian, Alec Prince, might be worth checking. Jank had suspected him of trapping another man's line as well as pilfering from unoccupied cabins. In fact, he had a feeling that Alec was somehow connected with the mysterious burning of Jack Blanchard's cabin the year before.

When the police trio swooped in for a ski landing at the Forks, among those waiting was trapper Ed Stranberg who turned over to the police a packsack he had found in a deserted cabin on the Ospika River. The cabin, said Stranberg, belonged to an Indian called Joe Pierre. But what made him pay attention to the packsack was the fact it had a special outside pocket to hold a camera. Stranberg had seen this packsack before — in Mesmer's cabin. Thinking it might offer some clue, the trapper had snowshoed 20 miles to turn it over to the police.

This news caused Jank to remember that Alec Prince used to stay in Pierre's cabin. The two were great friends. Jank quickly found Pierre, bundled him aboard the plane and flew to Ospika River to see what else the cabin would reveal. The plane didn't stay, but returned to the Forks to take Clark and McKenney to Fort Grahame where they interviewed Maguire and Ware. Apart from describing how they found Mesmer, the only other information they could offer was that a group of Indians had lately been congregating on Collins Creek. A quick check there disclosed that Alec Prince had stayed with them for four days. During his visit he showed one of them a gold watch.

Back once more at Finlay Forks, pilot Pat Carey left Clark and McKenney, then winged his way to Ospika River to return with Jank and Pierre. In Pierre's cabin had been a surprise for the policemen — tools, axes, guns, clothing and other items.

Pierre said it all belonged to Alec Prince. But the trappers and prospectors at the Forks had a different opinion. Much of it was identified as having been stolen in the last few months. Jack Blanchard was surprised to see articles he thought had gone up in flames in his cabin. One was a leather brief case which someone remembered Mesmer making. In the brief case was a gold watch and a few rolls of film.

Down on the river bank, searching through the Indian cabins, finally Clark and McKenney found Alec Prince. As a start, Jank arrested him under the Game Act for illegal trapping.

"Somebody said you had a couple of cameras," said Sergeant Clark to the swarthy youth. "Where are they?" The Indian shook his head.

In a cardboard box behind the stove, however, the policemen found the cameras, along with another watch and chain, plus some more film. Clark thereupon took possession of Prince's .30-30 rifle, along with its handsomely-beaded buckskin scabbard and a buckskin cartridge pouch.

"Never did I see a group nearer to a lynching." said Sergeant

Clark, when he referred later to Prince's arrest. "so I locked him up in a fur loft, and put McKenney on guard — just in case."

The solitide, apparantly, got Prince thinking. He said he wanted to see the Sergeant. Then through trapper Del Miller, a fluent Sikanee interpreter, he said that Mesmer had invited him into the cabin for a drink of lemon extract. In fact he had many drinks, until finally he didn't know what he was doing. Maybe he shot Mesmer, he didn't know. Anyway, Pfeuffer appeared and chased him away with a gun. It was either kill or be killed, so he shot Pfeuffer. He hung around, watching the injured man as he lay on the ice, until finally in the morning he possessed Pfeuffer's gun and threw it in the river through a hole in the ice.

A careful police investigation showed some discrepancy in the story. With Prince's background it was more likely that Mesmer came upon the Indian prowling the cabin, perhaps taking a watch, or the cameras. Whatever happened, one thing was evident — Mesmer had no chance for he was shot twice in the back. The lemon extract story was invalid since the supplies in the cabin were non-alcoholic. To make sure the police had them analysed, as well as the dregs in some empty bottles.

Clark felt that after Mesmer's death Pfeuffer had appeared and vengefully pursued the Indian. Finally Prince turned and fired at him, whereupon Pfeuffer retreated, the Indian after him. Knowing a determined killer was on his trail, it must have been with terrible desperation that Pfeuffer stumbled ahead on his snowshoes. Finally, the Indian shed his to pursue his victim on swift moccasined feet, narrowing the gap until he fired the shot that broke Pfeuffer's leg. Pfeuffer, rifle in hand, fell to the ice then vainly tried to claw his way to safety. By superhuman exertion he made the shelter of a log near the river bank.

Finally night fell, and so did the temperature. When morning broke the trapper was still alive, though by now incapable of movement. Only his eyes gave sign of life as they followed the Indian's movements. Finally, when Prince realized his victim was too weak to offer further resistance, he circled in like a wolf on a hamstrung deer. Finally, he was close enough to grab the rifle then drop it through a hole in the river ice.

At his trial that fall in Prince George, the non-alcoholic nature of the trapper's lemon extract, plus the accuracy of Prince's shooting, disposed of his plea that he was drunk. In addition, the bullet taken from Mesmer's body was fired from Prince's rifle.

The verdict was guilty. On November 29, 1944, at Oakalla Prison Prince was hanged.

George Varty, 14, was sentenced to
one year at hard labor for burglary.
One 11-year-old boy served six
months for "using profane language."

When Prisoners Weren't Pampered

**They varied in age from eight to nearly 100, their
main pastime was breaking rocks while wearing
heavy, rivetted-on shackles; and a staple food was
gruel which consisted of one part oatmeal to nine
parts of water.**

by Deputy Commissioner Cecil Clark

As historic sites go, I don't suppose there'll be any agitation to
mark the one-time location of Victoria's old Hillside Gaol — as jails
used to be called. When we British Columbians clear away the past
we make a job of it! There isn't a vestige of the 1900s-era jail, even
though a stone wall 13 feet high by two feet thick enclosed the
some 20-acre site.

The jail was built in 1886 and served the province until 1912
when it burned down. Today the site is occupied by S. J. Willis
School and the unmarked graves of five men who were hanged
there. Before being covered by the parking lot at the west end of
the school the outlines of rows of cells were evident. There were
70, each nine feet long by six feet wide, seven feet for women.
(They were palatial, however, compared with those in Ontario's
Kingston Jail which were like coffins. Each was 27-inches wide by
6½ feet long, a 24-inch wide bed hinged to the wall and a bible the
only furnishings.) Cells had no lights or water, the indoor plumbing consisting of a "cell bucket" which the prisoner emptied in the
morning.

Life in Hillside bastille was modelled on the "skilly and fetters"
pattern of similar institutions in Victorian England. The fetters
were leg irons. Each set consisted of two, three-foot-long iron links
which weighed 14 pounds. To discourage any thought of shedding
them they were rivetted around a prisoner's ankles when he entered the jail and laboriously removed with a hammer and chisel
when he was released — or hanged. At Kamloops jail in the 1890s
one hanging scheduled for 8 a.m. was delayed an hour because
chiselling off the thick iron rivets took two hours. During this time
the prisoner sat smoking "cigarette after cigarette."

Hillside Gaol and staff in 1892. In the center is Warden R. F. John who tried to improve the brutal conditions. The site today is a school, on the grounds the unmarked graves of men who were hanged.

Leg irons came in two sizes, 14 and 28 pounds. They were rivetted on and not removed until a prisoner finished the sentence. (See pages 20-21.)

43

The leg irons were chained to a heavy belt around the prisoner's waist. Although most uncomfortable, he still had to do the heavy manual labor which was a part of sentences. Manual labor meant exactly what the words indicated — with plenty of it. Work included cutting wood, building and repairing streets, and breaking rock with a sledge hammer. Unfortunately for the prisoners, there was no shortage of rock. It was sold for $2 a wagon load and provided the foundation for most of Victoria's downtown streets. On wet days the prisoners had the luxury of staying inside, and while they were dry, they weren't idle or gossiping since the rule was no talking. Instead of breaking rocks, they picked oakum. This oakum, smelling of tar, arrived in tightly rolled ropes. Prisoners had to laboriously tease it into loose bundles which were stuffed in sacks to be used in caulking the wooden naval ships.

The daily routine began at 5 a.m. when the cooks were aroused, although what they had to cook required little effort and no imagination. The Prisons' Regulations Act stipulated the menu for each meal. There were two scales. Scale Number One was for prisoners awaiting trial and those sentenced to hard labor for 30 days or less.

Scale Number Two was for prisoners doing hard labor for over 30 days. For breakfast these men were entitled to eight ounces of bread and one pint of gruel which could contain no more than two ounces of oatmeal. In other words, nine parts water to one part oatmeal, called "skilly" in English prisons where it was equally unpopular. Topping off the meal was one pint of "coffee" made from roasted ground peas, sweetened with molasses or brown sugar. After this hearty breakfast the work gangs, in shackles, were on the rockpile by 8 a.m.

They got an hour for dinner which consisted of six ounces of meat (without bone), eight ounces of bread and eight ounces of potatoes on each day that hard labor was performed. On the days when they didn't work, they were fed on Scale Number One.

This repast consisted of five ounces of cooked meat (without bone), eight ounces of bread, and eight ounces of potatoes for three days of the week. For two days it was eight ounces of bread, one pound of potatoes, and one pint of gruel. The other two days were much less bountiful — one pint of gruel and eight ounces of bread.

Supper at 5:30 was one pint of gruel and eight ounces of bread. But, as the Act noted "...all prisoners shall be allowed at their meals as much good water and salt as they desire."

No spirits of any kind was permitted in the jail, nor was tobacco "...except by order of the Gaol Surgeon, such order to be recorded in his Journal, together with the name of the prisoner to whom the privilege is allowed." Visiting hours were three and one-half hours on Saturday and two hours on Sunday, although even these were grudgingly given since "All visitors are requested to make their visits as brief as possible."

The cost of a prisoner's upkeep was a modest 9 cents a day, thanks to the regulation bread and gruel. But in the 1890s inflation set in and the cost of food soared to 13 cents a day. Adding overheads such as salaries and maintenance brought the total to 58 cents a day per prisoner, or about $212 a year. By contrast, today the cost is something like $50,000 a year.

About one-third of the prisoners couldn't read or write and their ages varied from eight to nearly 100. In 1895 two were 10 years old, one was 97. He was Frank Creagan, a snowy-bearded Irish patriarch who could be seen any summer day sitting on a bench in the jail yard, sucking a stubby clay pipe. Old Frank had served in the East India Company and seen the carnage of the Indian Mutiny with its Black Hole of Calcutta. He died in Victoria when he was well over 100.

Four of the prisoners are still buried on the grounds, their graves unknown. Convicted of murder, they were hanged. The first was Robert G. Sproule who could very well have been innocent. In 1885 Sproule was accused of shooting Thomas Hammill on the Blue Bell Mine at Galena Bay on Kootenay Lake. The resulting trial and its aftermath pitted brother against brother and spread not only across Canada to the Prime Minister but also to London and Washington.

After a lengthy trial in Victoria, Sproule was found guilty but the jury recommended mercy. In other words, they didn't feel that the death penalty was warranted. Nevertheless, Sproule was sentenced to hang. The battle for Sproule's life involved two of B.C.'s most notable lawyers. Prosecutor was Attorney-General A. B. Davie who was to become B.C. premier the next year. His brother, Theodore, defended Sproule and he, too, became a B.C. premier. After the death sentence, Theodore Davie fought desperately to save Sproule and managed to have his appointment with the hangman postponed seven times.

The arguments were aired right up to Canada's Supreme Court where Theodore Davie won a reprieve for the condemned man, and Mr. Justice Henry ordered Sproule to be set free. B.C.'s Attorney-General, A. B. Davie, however, was determined to have Sproule hanged despite the jury's recommendation for mercy and growing public opposition. He ignored the order to free Sproule. Instead he called for a special session of the Federal Supreme Court where Judge Henry's brother justices said he was wrong. Sproule was again scheduled for the hangman.

In Washington, the U.S. Secretary of State had become involved, writing to Sproule's father in Maine "... we will inquire into the matter. In the meantime rest assured that Canadian authority will no doubt take every possible action in order that justice may be done."

Sproule had now been reprieved six times but this time he seemed doomed. Nevertheless, lawyer Theodore Davie still fought to save him. Two days before the scheduled hanging he wired the Minister of Justice in Ottawa to postpone the execution to allow an appeal to the Privy Council in London. The Minister replied: "The law must be carried out. Sproule will be executed October 1, whether he appeals or not." To the Americans, this demonstration of Canadian justice mustn't have been reassuring.

Because of this continued dance with death, Sproule ate little of the prison food which, as noted, was essentially bread and gruel. Death had now passed by six times. Perhaps, however, the postponements were working for him since many people felt that the mental torture he had undergone was alone reason to justify commutation.

Then, incredibly, on the afternoon before his scheduled execution, the jailer again brought word of a reprieve — the seventh. Sproule would now hang on Friday, October 29.

"The coffin has been made, the rope is ready, and the scaffold erected," wrote editor D. W. Higgins in the *Victoria Colonist*. "And a telegram comes from Ottawa a mere 16 hours before the hanging…. It's a refinement of cruelty to hang him now."

The reason for the last-minute delay was that the U.S. State Department and the British Colonial Office were getting bombarded with disquieting rumors about a claim jumping case in B.C. Would Canada's Government take a second look at the case? Apparently Ottawa did, and on October 27 came the answer: Sproule would hang on October 29 as scheduled, the eighth death sentence.

When October 28 dawned in Ottawa, still one more interested person was to be heard from. He was Mayor Fell of Victoria who had paid his own expenses to go to Ottawa and present a petition from Victoria citizens. In brief, emotion-packed phrases, Fell told Canada's Prime Minister that a pardon or commutation was the hope of those he represented at the coast. It was no use. The law had to have its way.

On October 29, 1886, citizens who picked up their *Victoria Colonist* found the lead editorial headed "The Final Act." It went on to say: "Before these lines shall have reached the majority of our readers Robert Evans Sproule, whether guilty or guiltless of the murder of which he was convicted, will be beyond human aid….

"If he was guilty," the editorial continued, "then in deference to contrary opinion he should have had commutation."

It was all to no avail and Sproule mounted the scaffold in the Hillside Gaol at 8 o'clock on the morning of October 29, 1886. A short speech, a few words of prayer, and the black-hooded executioner touched the lever.

But for Sproule, even in death misfortune continued to embrace him. He requested burial on U.S. soil, but no one claimed him. As a consequence, he was buried in the jail yard "...below the hill on the south side."

Even being buried in foreign soil in a unmarked grave wasn't the last of Sproule's misfortune. A few days after his execution came word that in his native Maine he had won a long standing legal suit which today would be the equivalent of over $1 million.

But the most cruel aspect is that Sproule could well have been innocent. As the November 4, 1886, issue of the *New York Tribune* commented:

"The hanging of Robert Sproule at Victoria, B.C. entails a fearful responsibility on the Canadian government. Evidence of Sproule's innocence is so strong as to have convinced the public that he was wrongly convicted."

If Sproule was treated unfairly by the harsh judicial system of the late Nineteenth Century, he wasn't alone. Records show that convicts at Hillside as young as eight were sentenced to one year in its grim cells. I learned about this aspect of our judicial heritage when I visited Victoria's City Police Headquarters and saw Inspector Jim Smith, the Department's unofficial historian. He produced from his archives a leather-bound photo album with a brass clasp. Seems that just before the turn of the century, Superintendent Harry Shepherd had started taking mug shots to aid identification. As well as being a good idea it was a first for Western Canada, as was Victoria's Police Force which was born in July 1858, nine years before the Dominion of Canada.

As I turned the pages I was halted by a boy's face. He was a jug-eared kid who faced the camera a century ago with a look of wide-eyed innocence. In the style of the day his picture was mounted on a 3- x 5-inch card, his record on the back. His name was George Varty, he was 14, sentenced to a year at hard labor for burglary.

During the time Varty served his sentence in the juvenile reformatory section of Hillside, 24 boys were admitted or released. The youngest was eight, the oldest 17. Three of them — 12, 13 and 14 years old — were each doing two years for housebreaking or stealing.

Guy Emery, 10, did three months for stealing. No sooner was he out than he was back in again, this time with his brother, Harold, aged 8. Both were to serve 12 months for stealing.

The record shows that Albert Dick, aged 11, did six months for using profane language (one wonders what the judge would have thought about today's TV!) Then there was Edwin Coles, 13, a born criminal if ever there was one. He was serving 14 days for using a slingshot.

According to the Hillside Jail report, during Varty's sentence the daily routine for juveniles was:

7 a.m. Breakfast at the table. As each boy finishes breakfast he proceeds upstairs to the lavatory and empties his cell pail and washes, stripped to the waist, each in turn; he then shakes out his blankets and rolls them up. Each boy has then allotted to him the task, spelling, which will keep him occupied while the Superintendent is absent at breakfast.

8:00 to 9:30 - Learning lessons in cells. The Warden of the jail is informed of the departure of the Superintendent by signal on electric bell.

9:30 - Superintendent returns and conducts prayers, boys reading aloud in turn verse by verse of Psalms or Proverbs.

10:00 to 10:30 - Repeating lessons learned in cells.

10:30 to 11:45 - Arithmetic class.

12:00 - Noon dinner.

Interval for exercise and recreation in yard.

2:00 to 4:00 p.m. - Afternoon school, writing in copybooks, dictation.

4:00 to 4:45 - Interval. Quiet amusement in school room; sometimes a run in the yard.

5:00 - Supper

5:30 - Boys go to cells with reading books. Superintendent leaves, returning in the evening.

For variety, two boys each day were put to work scrubbing and sweeping, laying the tables for meals — although the spartan food required a minimum of utensils — removing ashes from the stove, carrying in coal and similar tasks.

Of the wardens, the best known was R. F. John, a somewhat forward looking official who did his best to improve the standards of Victorian prisons. But he would never have been able to imagine the changes that would occur over subsequent years.

During his day eight-year-old Harold Emery was given one year in an unlighted cell with a bucket for a toilet for minor theft. By contrast as I type these words the radio has just announced that in Manitoba a 13-year-old boy who brutally knifed to death two women — one was 59, the other was 86 — received three years. His time will be served in a detention center which includes excellent meals, central heating, with plumbing, electric lights and TV. Again, in contrast to young Harold Emery, scores of murderers walk free after serving less than five years for their crime.

Although the penal system as represented by Hillside Jail was harsh and brutal by our standards, it reflected public opinion of the day.

My First Northern Patrol

Among lessons that Constable B. E. Munkley quickly learned on his first solo into the wilderness was to make sure that boots fit and travel light — very light!

During the years that I was stationed in Northern B.C., I made numerous patrols into the bush. Some were arduous, and some were easy, but on every one I had experiences that I will always remember. I think that one of the most memorable was my first patrol into the bush alone.

It was while I was stationed at Terrace, a community on the Skeena River approximately 90 miles east of Prince Rupert, that I received instructions to proceed into the Nass Valley, about 75 miles north of Terrace. My orders were to investigate a complaint about a settler who had gone insane and had taken several shots at another settler. I received the instructions with mixed feelings. I was anxious to make the trip, but never had been on such a trip before, and certainly not alone. I spent a very busy day gathering what I considered essential for the patrol. Not being accustomed to outfitting, I bought a large assortment of food, a good 75 per cent of which was unnecessary, and built my pack on to a Trapper Nel-

Constable B. E. Munkley and his huge pack on his first patrol. It weighed 85 pounds, about 50 more, he discovered, than he needed.

son packboard. When my pack was completed, I found that I had 85 pounds. After discarding everything that I considered non-essential, I still had 80 pounds, plus an 11-pound rifle and a small axe.

On September 14, 1940, I left Terrace and had a car transport me — and my huge pack — to the end of the road at Kitsumgallum Lake. Bidding farewell to the other Constable who was to take my place while I was away, I proceeded up the lake to a cabin occupied by telegraph lineman Walter Warner and his wife. The couple made me welcome and insisted that I spend the night with them. I saw Warner eyeing my bulging pack, but at the time I thought nothing of it. Since that time, I realize that he must have thought that I would learn a lot better by experience than by anything he said.

I spent a very interesting evening with the Warners and received directions as to the trail. He also warned me to be careful while crossing a large field of lava rock where the trail was not discernible.

I got an early start in the morning and headed up the trail at a brisk walk, intending to reach a deserted telegraph cabin 15 miles north before making camp for the night. I estimated that I should arrive there at approximately 2 p.m. I had, however, underestimated the length of the miles and the weight of the pack, to say nothing of my physical condition. The trail was quite rocky over undulating country and, to make matters worse, I discovered that my boots were too small. With the weight of my big pack and considerable walking up and down in under-sized boots, it wasn't long before my feet began to hurt. After many rests, I reached the 15-mile cabin at about 4 p.m.

The cabins on this telegraph line were very old and quite small, as they were used only on rare occasions by linemen. On opening the door I observed a large heap of dried green leaves piled almost roof high on the bunk, and a very objectionable odor. I later found that the smell and leaves were attributable to bush, or pack, rats, the curse of the trapper and prospector in the north. However, like the advantages in travelling light, pack rats were something else with which I was unfamiliar.

I prepared a fine supper of canned stew and even had a dessert. Being very tired, I went to bed at sunset after bathing my aching feet in a nearby creek. I immediately fell into an exhausted sleep. Some time during the night I awoke with a start to find a small animal had been chewing my hair, apparently to obtain the salt from perspiration. Not knowing what I was facing, I reached for my high-powered rifle and flashlight (yes, I even had that) and sat motionless in the dark, the rifle to my shoulder and the flashlight held along the barrel. I heard a movement in the corner of the cabin, flashed the light, and on seeing two eyes, pulled the trigger. I quickly learned another lesson — never fire a rifle in a very small cabin.

The blast was deafening and I thought for a moment that my ear drums had burst. Several tin cans fell off shelves to add to the din. I did get my animal though, or what was left of it. I didn't recognize the type, but did realize what had caused the rank odor in the cabin. I returned to my bunk confident that I had handled that situation with dispatch. It was not so. I had no more sleep that night. There proved to be several other bush rats using the same home, and I learned something else — they can make a lot of noise with their hind feet. Once or twice I dozed off to sleep only to awaken with a start when a rat thumped his feet.

After a substantial breakfast the next morning, I started to roll up my pack but decided to lighten my huge load by leaving out a few cans for the return trip. I cached several in the cabin and after cleaning out the debris, set out for another cabin about 25 miles distant. I had travelled only a few miles when I realized that my night's rest had not left me very refreshed. My feet started to hurt and the pack seemed to be gaining weight. The rifle I was carrying was awkward, so I carefully roped it on to my pack in order to keep my hands free. I was soon to learn another lesson about woods travel.

During the afternoon I was going over a pass which rose to about 1,500 feet, the trail overgrown with thick young spruce trees. They made walking difficult and the only way to get through was to put my head down and push.

On breaking into a clearing, I ran right into a medium-sized grizzly bear feeding on berries. Startled by my appearance, it rose up on its hind feet and snorted. But if the bear was startled, I was not. I was scared stiff.

My rifle was securely tied on my pack and there I was, rooted to the spot. I believe that is what saved me. The bear watched me for a few seconds and then dropped on all fours and ambled away. I forthwith took my rifle off the packboard and sat down for a cigarette. In fact, I smoked several before I felt able to travel.

I camped that night in a cabin on the shore of a pretty lake. I again recognized the bush rat smell in this cabin but was too tired to care. I had a reasonable amount of sleep. But when I got up in the morning I found that the rats had stolen my knife and fork that I had left on a small table, and no amount of searching revealed the hiding place. Another lesson in bushcraft. I now knew why they were called pack rats.

I again cached a quantity of canned foods and started on my way. During this day I reached the long stretch of lava rock the Warners had mentioned. While crossing the lava I had to skirt a gully that had been washed out by a spring freshet. Being very tired, I did not exercise caution. I lost my footing and tumbled into the gully — big pack, rifle and all, stunning myself.

When I came to, I found that my right ankle was badly sprained, and I was severely bruised and shaken. I still had 12 miles to travel and walking that distance was certainly difficult in my battered condition. I was afraid to drop my still huge pack in case I couldn't carry on.

Towards dark by sheer good fortune I stumbled into a farm yard where an elderly woman, bent double from hard work, was busy at a woodpile. I asked for a drink of water. After one look she hustled me inside her cabin and made me lie down while she got me a drink of water. I was ordered to take off my boots while she produced a tub of hot water and a roll of homemade bandages. When I removed my too-small boots I found that both big toenails were loose. I was to experience for months afterwards the discomfort caused when both nails dropped off. Mrs. X bound my injured ankle and made me rest. When Mr. X came in I was amazed at his size and appearance. He was well over six feet tall and as erect as a ramrod, with a grand beard. I was to learn later that he was over 70. The couple were Scots and their hospitality was embarrassing as I could see that they were in needy circumstances. I shared their frugal meal and found that they had no sugar. I knew that I would offend them if I offered to give them some so I made a deal. I gave them five pounds of sugar for a night's lodging. (Why I was packing five pounds of sugar for one man on a week-long patrol I have often wondered.)

Later in the evening when I was discussing conditions in the Nass Valley with Mr. X the realization gradually dawned on me that he was the reported mental case. Worse, hanging above the bunk on which he was sitting was a rack containing several guns. To all appearances, however, both appeared to be industrious and hard-working settlers, and certainly did not give the impression of being mental patients. I was amazed at his knowledge of world affairs considering that he was situated in such a remote area without even a radio. Later that evening I explained the reason for my patrol and, tongue in cheek, awaited his reaction. It came quickly. He roared with laughter, in fact the cabin fairly rocked. By contrast, his wife was quite indignant about the complaint having brought the poor "pollis man" all the way into that area for no good reason.

He explained that one of his neighbors had built a fence across his trail to the trading post, thereby forcing him to travel a considerable distance farther when going for provisions. He had finally rebelled and cut the fence. He assured me that had he ever found it necessary to shoot at anyone, he wouldn't miss.

The next morning, the Manager of the Trading Post at Aiyansh arrived at the farm on horseback. When he learned of my injured foot he insisted that I take his horse to carry my pack to Aiyansh. He advised me not to ride the horse with my pack as it was only a very small Indian cayuse. I winced at his unspoken criticism, glad that he hadn't seen the pack before I got rid of some canned goods and the five pounds of sugar.

On my arrival at Aiyansh I learned that it consisted of a Post Office and Trading Post run by Mr. and Mrs. Gray. I received a cordial invitation to stay with them during my patrol over the area to register firearms. It was indeed a home away from home at the Grays. They loaned me a saddle horse for my patrol and I was able to cover the entire valley during my stay. I certainly enjoyed visiting the various homesteaders in the district. It was a district as fertile and productive as any in B.C. but without any method of getting produce to the markets.

When I had completed my mission, I found that my ankle was still badly swollen. I began making enquiries to find an easier way of getting out as I knew the trail was out of the question. After some difficulty, I arranged with an Indian who was going down the Nass River to Prince Rupert to take me with him and his family. Mrs. Gray made me a wonderful lunch of fried chicken and sandwiches, and we set out in the Indian's gillnet boat. It was a beautiful trip down the river and one that I certainly will never forget. An amusing incident occurred during the trip down river. When it came time for lunch, the Indian women prepared their lunch. Seeing that I had mine, they gave me a cup of tea. I unwrapped the chicken and proceeded to eat it in the time-honored manner of picking it up with my fingers. I certainly did not make a very favorable impression on the Indians who immediately turned their backs to me.

We arrived at Prince Rupert early the next morning. I returned to Terrace later that same day by train, having been away on patrol for 10 days.

During the following year, I gained considerable experience in bush travel. I was subsequently transferred to Port Essington, near the mouth of the Skeena River. While stationed there I was instructed to return to Terrace and again proceed to the Nass Valley as some further trouble required attention. With the aid of previous experience, I was able to walk in to the Valley , clear up the trouble and walk out again in less than six days, with no ill effects. My pack on the second patrol weighed 32 pounds.

I had learned by experience.

Some were clean, others shunned water except for drinking; some were normal, others mentally unstable; some lived in comfortable cabins, others in hovels. They were the

Hinterland Hermits

by Deputy Commissioner Cecil Clark

Patrolling the little-known parts of B.C.'s Interior, policemen and Game Wardens occasionally ran across some strange characters. They were men not to be confused with the trapper or prospector who usually preserved the amenities of civilization.

I refer to the type who shun society, isolating themselves from the world. Take, for instance, a man encountered by Game Inspector George Stevenson years ago on a little frequented tributary of the Squamish River. Living alone in a veritable hovel, he was apparently of middle age, and bore in addition a name that had spattered the pages of English history. Although he was obviously well educated, a skillet and a sack of flour seemed to sum up his fundamental food requirements. On Stevenson's short visit he formed the opinion that the voluntary exile was an authority on two subjects: Shakespeare and the fallacy of washing. Though he drank the nearby river water, there apparently its usefulness ended for he pleasantly affirmed he hadn't washed or bathed in years!

Another case was a man Constable Bob Pritchard told me about years ago. When he was posted to Sicamous in the early 1920s, he discovered that part of his patrol area, just part mind

This packing-crate sized cabin was home to a Peace River hermit.

When travelling through Tweedsmuir Park while he was Governor-General of Canada, Lord Tweedsmuir, second from left, met a boyhood friend turned recluse.

you, was the 600-mile-long shoreline of Shuswap Lake. There being no roads or trails, Bob covered one of B.C.'s largest lakes in a small boat. Sailing and rowing, that is. There were no motors.

One day he got word that an old Polish character living alone hadn't been seen all winter. Bob set out to see if he was dead or alive. He had previously heard by rumor something of the man's history. Apparently he had once been an expert fur cutter in a big Eastern city and over the years several big fur dealers had sought him out with high priced offers to return to his trade. He constantly rejected these offers.

When Pritchard finally landed at his beach he could see that there hadn't been any boat traffic for a long time. Then when he encountered a couple of trees down across the trail, he naturally thought that Father Time had caught up with the lonely bush dweller.

Eventually Pritchard reached the cabin and knocked on the door. There was no answer. He tried the latch but found the door barricaded on the inside. He was trying to force the door when a sepulchral voice demanded. "Who's there?"

"A friend," yelled Pritchard, "open the door." He stepped nimbly aside, expecting a rifle or a shotgun blast as had been known to happen.

After a long pause the door creaked slowly open to reveal the strangest looking man the policeman had ever seen. He was old, very old, frail and undernourished. A white beard draped his chest, matching the hair that cascaded to his shoulder blades. His clothing was a robe of flour sacks, and showed signs of having been patched and repatched. When the policeman stepped into the cabin's gloomy interior, his first spoken thought was about the state of the man's larder.

In answer the hermit pointed to a couple of sacks of flour and half a case of canned milk. As Pritchard discovered him singularly uncommunicative and apparently in no mood for visitors, he cut short his visit. However, as he was leaving, he idly asked the old man how he had put in his time during the winter.

The man gave him a rheumy-eyed stare and a one-word answer: "Meditating." Apparently he weathered a few more years of "meditation" for he was still alive when Pritchard was transferred to another post.

Bob also told me of another solitary Shuswap Lake dweller at the head of Anstey Arm who aroused his interest. This man was a Russian trapper who, according to rumor, had a violent argument with one French Louie about trapping rights. According to the grape vine, the argument had gone further than words.

Anyway, after a long winter finally made way for spring, one man wasn't around to enjoy the change. French Louie had vanished.

At first, Constable Pritchard had great difficulty in even finding the missing man's cabin. When finally he succeeded it was obvious that it hadn't been occupied all winter. Then came a report from a Forest Ranger that the mysterious Russian seemed to be discouraging people from landing on his beach. His method was very effective — sitting on the shore with a loaded rifle across his knees.

Pritchard naturally investigated. When he hauled his boat up, there was the Russian with his rifle. Bob, however, wasn't impressed. He proceeded to give him some forceful advice about firearms and Canadian law, then asked to see his trapper's licence.

Though the Russian had the reputation of never allowing anyone to enter his cabin, again Bob wasn't impressed. Besides, he had a special interest in seeing the interior. He thought it might contain something belonging to French Louie.

He found to his surprise, however, that it was not only neat and clean, but well supplied with provisions. The construction, he noted, was away above average, and the homemade furniture could have easily graced a city showroom. The licence was in order, then the Russian produced some marten pelts and a couple of grizzly bear skins, showing evident signs of expert treatment.

As Pritchard took in his surroundings, he couldn't help feeling there was something strange and mysterious about the whole setup. For one thing, the cabin had been built on a promontory around which all the trees had been felled, apparently to give a good view up and down the lake. For another, at the back was a lookout in a tree where, apparently, the Russian spent hours watching and waiting. For what though? Or whom?

About a week later Constable Pritchard returned with an assistant. Together they dragged the lake for three days for trace of French Louie. Not a clue did they find, nor did he turn up anywhere else. In fact his disappearance is still a mystery.

Some years after Frenchy's disappearance, the Russian followed the pattern of so many bush dwellers. He became unbalanced and was committed to a mental hospital. There he eventually died, taking his secret with him.

Another case involving a recluse was told to me by Leslie Jeeves who spent a lifetime as a policeman, retiring as an RCMP Inspector. Les was stationed at Cranbrook in his early Provincial Police career. From there he journeyed one day to visit an old Scotsman who lived alone near Ta Ta Creek. The old-timer eked a meagre living from a one-man mine he ran near his cabin, his only companion an aged horse that hauled a stone-boat to bring out ore.

The cabin was empty when Jeeves arrived so he headed down the trail to the mine. He heard voices, then recognized it was the miner talking to his horse. Rounding a bend in the trail, he saw an astonishing sight. The man was hauling the stone-boat with leather traces over his shoulders, and the horse was looking on!

When Jeeves introduced himself the recluse explained that the horse was too old to haul the load, so he just brought him along for company.

As they talked Jeeves quickly realized that though the old man was friendly enough, he was not only mentally unbalanced but also in very poor health.

Jeeves eventually persuaded him to lock his cabin, leave the horse with a neighbor and accompany him to Cranbrook. There, two doctors booked him into a mental hospital at the Coast. By chance, Jeeves got the job of escorting him to New Westminster.

Up to this time, Jeeves had typed him as "tractable but bushed" — a description that fitted until the train made a stop. Among the new passengers was a Chinese, who took a seat near the policeman and his charge.

As soon as the miner noticed the Chinese he gave one screech and promptly fell on him. Jeeves had to exert all of his well-known brawn to separate the pair before the inoffensive Chinese got strangled. What triggered the violent outburst Jeeves never knew.

A hermit story with a strange twist of coincidence was told by the late T. W. S. "Tom" Parsons, one-time head of the B.C. Provincial Police. It happened in the late 1930s when 5,400 square miles of scenic wilderness was set aside as Tweedsmuir Park.

To launch the project in proper style, Lord Tweedsmuir (John Buchan) then Governor-General of Canada, was invited to visit the park. Among various officials in the vice-regal packhorse expedition which wound its way from Burns Lake to the Bella Coola Valley in the Coast Mountains was Commissioner Parsons.

One evening, after a lakeside supper, Parsons suggested to the Governor-General that a stroll along a nearby sandbar, in the full glory of a majestic sunset, would perhaps be a fitting way to end the day.

The two men had much in common. Parsons had been in the South African Constabulary about the same time that John Buchan was secretary to Lord Milner, then Governor at the Cape. Talking and walking, they moved slowly along the sandbar until Parsons noticed a shack built of slabs of bark and sodded over. Since it was the merest apology for shelter, he decided it had probably been someone's temporary abode years before.

To his surprise, however, when they got within 30 feet of the ramshackle structure from it appeared an old and somewhat decrepit character. By his straggly locks and beard, coupled with a hooked nose and piercing glance, he reminded Parsons of someone out of the Old Testament.

For a moment the strange fellow stood, forbiddingly eyeing the approaching strangers. Then, when about 10 feet separated them, suddenly his eyes kindled with the light of recognition. Taking a step forward he stretched out his hand to the Governor-General.

"Why," he said with a wheezy chuckle that accompanied his broad Scots, "if it isnae' wee Johnny! Wee Johnny Buchan himsel'. Mon, I'd ken ye onywhaur!"

As the incongruous pair shook hands, Police Commissioner Parsons wondered what had happened to the traditional protocol surrounding a meeting with the Governor-General. Lord Tweedsmuir promptly solved the mystery by introducing the recluse as one of his boyhood companions from Fifeshire, Scotland.

A boyhood companion it seemed, so isolated that he was quite unaware that "wee Johnny" was not only a peer but Canada's Governor-General. Just another example of some of the lonely bush dwellers who preferred the solitude of wilderness B.C. to what the rest of us call civilization.

Somewhere in the wilderness north of Fort St. John
trapper Brown distilled his illegal "joy water."

Leaving home at 2 a.m. Christmas morning on horseback in -30°F weather to search for a "moonshiner," then being three days overdue was all part of

A Police Christmas

by Inspector C. G. Barber

I shall always remember the Christmas of 1924. I was on detachment at Fort St. John in the Peace River District. At that time the Peace River block, particularly north of the river, was a straggling homesteading settlement. There were sufficient ladies in the settlement to make the occasional dance a worthwhile gathering, but as time went on I noticed that the excess of good spirits was not due alone to the entertainment. Investigating, I learned that the illegal "joy water" was produced by a trapper named Brown. By a coincidence, in former years he had excelled in the art of moonshining in the hills of Old Kentucky. He had migrated to the Peace River, and finding none too good a market for his grain, had hit upon the idea of turning some of it into alcohol.

My task was to find out where, in that vast expanse of country, his still was located. I concluded it must be on his trap line. Then I got in touch with Constable Forfar at Hudson Hope Detachment and asked him to meet me at Fort St. John. Forfar had 60 miles to travel on horseback and he arrived at dark on Christmas Eve.

Christmas was the day that meant so much to the bachelors of the district, and my wife and I had invited a number in for Christmas dinner. As I took my departure at two o'clock Christmas morning, I assured my better half that I would be back by evening. Under bright moonlight, the temperature dipping to -30°F, Forfar and I left with two saddle horses.

We hit the trail in a westerly direction past the end of Charlie Lake and followed the Hudson Hope trail for about four miles in a westerly direction. Then we waited for daylight at 9 o'clock so we could pick up the trail to Brown's trap line, which was supposed to branch off in a northerly direction. At daylight we searched for the trail without result. Then it dawned upon us that Brown had given false information when applying for his trapping licence. We retraced our steps to the lake, searching carefully for any trail leading off through the bush. We found none, and arrived back at the lake at two in the afternoon.

It now started snowing heavily, but we were determined not to give up. We followed the rim of the lake in a northerly direction for about eight miles, then came across a cache of empty bottles in a box on the lake shore. In the bush nearby were two old log buildings. One had been used as a stable, the other as a bunk house. A search of the buildings revealed nothing, but in the gathering dusk of the northern afternoon we discerned a trail leading from the lake in a northwest direction. It was fast becoming obliterated by the heavy fall of snow, so we decided to wait for daylight.

The buildings were roofed with swamp grass, and some of it underneath was in fair condition. I tore part of the roof off to feed the horses — they didn't relish it much. We had neither food nor blankets, and unlimited time to reflect upon the Christmas dinner we were missing.

After a wearisome night, dawn came to a cold, stark world outside. I fed the horses some more roof and, breakfastless, Forfar and I proceeded to pick up the trail we had seen the night before. It was difficult owing to the heavy snow, but we followed it for two miles, then lost it altogether. I learned later that, had it not been for the heavy snowfall obliterating the trail, we could have followed it right to the cabin we were seeking. We retraced our steps to the lake, saddled up and went on another six miles to the head of the lake. We found a trapper's cabin, but not the trapper we were seeking.

Here again was a building that had been used as a stable, roofed with swamp grass. We tore off some for the horses. Fortunately, in the cabin were a few staple articles of food. Forfar and I broke our fast for the first time in 24 hours. That evening, to further help the situation, a freighting team pulled in from the Fort Nelson trail and they were able to spare us a few oats and some butter, jam, etc. This made up a little for missing our Christmas dinner. The following morning, the second day after Christmas, we followed a trap line through heavy, snow-laden bush. At noon we discovered it was owned by a man named Paul Gladys, who had nothing to do with the moonshining business.

We were a dejected-looking pair when we got back to our starting point just after dusk. During our absence the trapper, Slim Estas, had returned from spending Christmas in the settlement. At the sight of the snow-bedecked men and horses he nearly collapsed, not so much from our weird appearance but from the fact that we were police officers. He knew what we were after.

I asked him to make some coffee, and we put the horses in and fed them a little roof covering. After they were as comfortable as circumstances would allow, we went into the cabin. We got out of our snow-covered, frozen outer garments and the warmth of the cabin was certainly appreciated. After coffee and bannock we felt more comfortable, but I could see that Slim was not.

He tried to put more wood in the stove than was really necessary, then in his uneasy wanderings he knocked over the water bucket. He picked it up, saying he was going to the spring for another pail. Thinking he was a long time gone I went out to look for him. There stood the pail, no Slim. In the bright moonlight I could see where he had ploughed through the snow. Following his tracks I finally circled around on to the hard-beaten trail on the lake where it was impossible to follow further by moonlight.

At daylight we saddled up and struck off down the lake, picking up Slim's tracks occasionally on the hard-beaten trail. After three miles, the trail turned at a right angle through the timber. No trouble now to follow his trail, but there was plenty of trouble trying to get the horses through the snow-laden underbrush and windfalls. The going was miserable, but after three miles we came to a small cabin near a spring and the smell of mash was strong in the frosty air. Alas, the birds had flown and taken their still with them.

I took a sample of the mash, but there was not sufficient liquid in it to determine whether it was mash suitable for making illicit liquor. However, I later got a conviction against Brown for giving false information when applying for a trapper's licence. At least I had the satisfaction of letting the moonshiners know that we were not afraid to tackle trails without food or shelter — even miss a good Christmas dinner.

In the B.C. Provincial Police, boots, caps, tunics and other apparel had a definite period of wear. If replacement was required earlier the reason had to be solid or the officer had to pay. Here is Sergeant Clark's explanation for his request:

"May I Be Supplied With A New Cap?"

by Deputy Commissioner Cecil Clark

George Clark, a friend of mine for years, was a tall, dark and rugged First World War veteran who won the Military Cross with Vancouver's 72nd Seaforths. In addition to bravery, another abiding

Sergeant George H. Clark, left, Special Constable "Skook" Davidson and Constable J. M. Russell at Fort Ware.

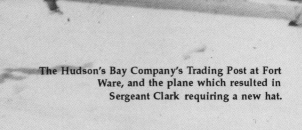

The Hudson's Bay Company's Trading Post at Fort Ware, and the plane which resulted in Sergeant Clark requiring a new hat.

characteristic was a strong sense of humor. He served, Constable to Inspector, for 30 years in the B.C. Police. Commissioned later in the RCMP, he was finally an Edmonton city magistrate.

Most of his B.C. Police service was in the north. Two of his memorable experiences occurred at Prince Rupert and Prince George. In Prince Rupert in 1939 he engaged in a shoot-out with a man who had brutally murdered two policemen. Clark, an expert marksman, won easily, hitting the pistol-toting murderer between the eyes. (See "The Parking Ticket That Killed Three People" in *B.C. Provincial Police Stories — Volume One.*)

Sergeant Clark's second memorable experience occurred in 1943. That January while stationed at Prince George he got a wire telling of a murder at Fort Ware, a lonely, snow-bound outpost 350 miles farther north. So lonely, in fact, that an Indian had to snow-shoe 80 miles to Finlay Forks so the Hudson's Bay man there could radio the message to his opposite number at Hazelton, who in turn put it on the land line to Prince George. Thus news of the northern tragedy travelled some 750 miles to reach Sergeant Clark.

In addition, reaching the isolated, roadless outpost wasn't easy, in either winter or summer. As a consequence, it wasn't until three weeks later that Sergeant Clark, along with Game Warden A. Jank, and Special Constable "Skook" Davidson took off in a Fairchild airplane piloted by veteran bush pilot Pat Carey. (Skook Davidson, who was a wartime buddy of Clark's, had won the Military Medal, Distinguished Conduct Medal and Bar, and the Croix de Guerre. After the war, he became a guide-outfitter in Northern B.C. and a legendary figure. See page 74.)

As the plane roared off into the frozen wilderness, pilot Carey viewed the sky with tight-lipped apprehension. He had reason to worry. Soon after takeoff the ceiling closed in to zero. Finally, there was nothing for it but to take a chance and put the plane down at Fort St. James. There the party remained stormbound for the next three days.

With a break in the weather they zoomed off again for Finlay Forks, to land on the frozen Finlay River for fuel. Here they found the drums of gasoline deep in drifted snow. Digging one out, they rolled it to the plane, and took turns pumping the fuel by hand.

When the aircraft took off once more, ceiling was so low that Carey had to virtually skim up the frozen river to Fort Ware. When they arrived it was around 11 o'clock on the morning of February 4, 24 days after the round-about telegram arrived at Prince George.

Fort Ware consisted of a Hudson's Bay Store, a fur cache and warehouse, and a cabin for stopover trappers. Nearby, another cabin housed store manager Jack Copeland, his wife and two children. As the police party clambered from the plane, Copeland greeted them with the warning that his latest weather report by radio didn't sound too good. He suggested they hurry their investigation if they didn't want to get snowed in. Taking the advice, Clark quickly got these facts.

It seemed that Stephen Poole of the Beaver tribe, returning home over the river ice one night in early January, in a drunken rage had clubbed his wife to death with a rifle butt. Leaving her on the ice, he stumbled home to sleep.

Next morning he retrieved her body, later telling those around the post she had frozen to death. Viewing the body they thought otherwise. Hence the message to the police. Poole's 10-year-old boy Tommy was apparently a witness to the crime.

Meantime, Clark learned, the body had been buried and now Poole was out on his trap line. Checking over the Indian's cabin, Clark took possession of the blood-stained rifle, then arranged for Skook Davidson to stay behind. He would collect the remaining witnesses and detain Poole when he came in with his fur. Then, to beat the approaching storm front, they hurriedly boarded the plane and took off. But as events turned out, they would have been much better off to stay at Fort Ware.

Their flight to the fuelling base at Finlay Forks was uneventful, then came misfortune heaped upon misfortune. As they were fuelling, snow began to fall.

Nothing for it but to stay the night, Clark and Carey bunking in with trapper Mort Teare, and the pilot and Jank occupying a vacant nearby cabin. Next morning, the flakes were coming down thicker than ever. Later in the day a local phenomenon known as a "Peace River Wind" started to funnel down the canyon. (The term "wind" was a typical northern understatement — elsewhere it would have been called a hurricane.) As it picked up velocity, the snowbound travellers began to wonder whether the plane would be blown down the ice.

Finally, in the teeth of the blizzard, they floundered through the drifts to anchor the aircraft with cables attached to full drums of gasoline. In addition, after great effort, they managed to lash a canvas covering over the engine and wings.

For five more weary days the wind howled, the cabin occupants only venturing out for stove wood and snow to melt for water. For Sergeant Clark, however, the time wasn't a total waste. Mort Teare told him of an incident which had resulted in the murder of a Special Constable north of Kamloops in 1907. (See next Chapter.) At last, when the wind slackened, Carey and his passengers had to plow through massive drifts to find the plane.

It was completely covered. But digging it out proved even harder.

Eventually, they set out two blow pots on the ice and started to warm the engine oil, drained from the motor when they first landed. When it was steaming they hastily poured it back and Carey stepped on the starter. Without result. As the whine of the starter grew more and more lethargic, it was a sure sign that the oil was congealing. A makeshift canvas tent was quickly rigged around the motor. All night long Carey worked on the engine, blow pots trying to ward off the sub-zero cold while a gale howled through the aircraft's rigging.

When morning dawned they were no nearer success. Carey felt that the oil wasn't thin enough. They'd drain it and heat it up. Then he made another startling discovery. The cylinder head was cracked.

Fortunately, Finlay Forks had the radio and Carey promptly reported his plight. Back came the comforting word that another cylinder head would be flown in. But their enthusiasm vanished in a blanket of white. For the next three days the weather was so bad no plane could be expected.

Their hopes rose with word that a plane had left Edmonton with the cylinder head. Again their enthusiasm was fleeting. Word followed that the plane had been diverted to a more pressing emergency — it had to join the hunt for a missing plane, down somewhere in the Peace River Country.

From then on, with intermittent blizzards, the party continued the role of wilderness prisoners. They lived on flapjacks and bacon, playing interminable games of cribbage during the long, long northern nights. A week passed, then on the tenth day they received news that a plane would try to reach them the next day.

Again Carey and his passengers, with the ever-willing trapper, Mort Teare, fought their way through the snow to the Fairchild. Here they discovered what a 60-mile-an-hour wind could do. The plane — and its anchoring gas drums — had been moved a hundred yards along the ice. In addition, the snow banked against it had taken on the consistency of concrete. It took them from dawn to dark to free the plane so that it could attempt a take off.

Toward noon the next day they heard a faint thrumming from over a snowclad peak. Finally, a speck appeared. As it grew they recognized it as another Fairchild. As soon as it landed, the precious cylinder head was handed to Carey, while the rescue plane whisked the police party to Prince George.

At his office, now 40 days since the telegram had arrived, Sergeant Clark made arrangements for an inquest. But because of the lack of space in the aircraft, he had to double-up on duties. Magistrate Bill Harris also became the coroner. Then there was trouble getting a doctor, but finally Captain J. C. Dawson, medical officer at a nearby army camp, was borrowed.

It was March 2 when Skook Davidson radioed from Fort Ware that he had Poole under arrest. Promptly the magistrate, the doctor,

Constable J. M. Russell, Indian Agent Bob Howe and Clark boarded the plane. Since there was a mechanic with the pilot, it made a hefty load. This trip, however, proved uneventful.

As soon as they arrived at Fort Ware, Margaret Poole's body was exhumed and Dr. Dawson performed a post mortem. Being frozen solid the body was in a perfect state of preservation though, as Sergeant Clark reported in an understatement, "rather hard to manipulate." Throughout this proceeding, her husband sat on a fence a few feet distant, stoically observing all that went on.

In one of the log cabins the jury was sworn in. After the evidence was heard all but the jury clumped outside. One of the last to leave tossed back the suggestion that they make it snappy. The weather again looked ominous.

With the jury's pronouncement, Poole was arrested. That night in the same building Magistrate Harris conducted a preliminary hearing and Poole was committed for trial.

About 11:30 that same night as they filed out of the building, Poole quietly remarked to Constable Russell: "What about Margaret? Suppose she stop there all night ... mebbe wolves eat her!"

It was a reminder that, in the haste of commencing the inquest, the body of the murdered woman had been left in its open pine coffin. It was still on the hilltop clearing that served as a cemetery. After brief consultation, the magistrate and the doctor, along with Clark and Skook Davidson, made their way up the hill.

There they put the lid back on the coffin. Then they lowered the simple casket into the grave and shovelled back the frozen earth.

It was after midnight when the burial party straightened from their labors and had a chance to look around. Here and there they glimpsed the tops of rude crosses dotting the heavy blanket of snow and at the edge of the clearing a barrier of pines, their branches weighed down with snow. In the distance the ice-capped mountains shone in the ghostly light of the cold northern moon. Coupled with the ghastly appearance of the woman they had just put underground it was, as Sergeant Clark said later, like something from the pen of Edgar Allan Poe.

Skook Davidson finally broke the silence, "Well," said the much decorated veteran, "let's give her a soldier's farewell."

He drew his gun and solemnly fired six shots in the air. Followed then a gesture that northerners could well appreciate. From the pocket of his peajacket, Sergeant Clark produced a mickey of rum. Wordlessly it passed from hand to hand to quick extinction.

Turning from the mound of earth, slowly and silently the quartet plodded down over the snow-covered trail to the river. As they did so, far back in the foothills a timber wolf mournfully howled for its mate. "Requiem for Margaret Poole," was Clark's comment to Bill Harris.

If the Fairchild had come up with a capacity load, it went back dangerously overloaded. Crowded aboard was not only the magistrate, the doctor, three policemen and the Indian Agent, but also the accused and his two children.

During take-off they almost crashed. After a long run down the ice, the plane veered and nearly piled up on the rock-studded river's edge. However, the passengers quickly piled out and pushed it back to mid-stream, or, more correctly, mid-ice.

Under full throttle the plane again thundered down the ice and finally started a slow climb — a very slow climb. There was a breathtaking moment when the skis skimmed the tops of the trees, then the pilot banked southward. But their problems weren't over. Heavy winds tossed them about the sky the entire way. George Clark later commented that it was the roughest trip he ever experienced. It was so windy they couldn't land at Finlay Forks and had to continue to McLeod Lake. Since most of the passengers had been violently airsick, the stop was welcome.

The snow on the lake was deep and soft, so this time for the take-off the plane had to be pushed around until its skis fitted the tracks made when landing. The Indians were pressed into service, though their only reward was to be engulfed in a propeller-blown blizzard. To take advantage of a strong tail wind, Carey made for Fort St. James for an overnight stop. Next morning the plane was back in Prince George.

The case, however, was still beset by problems peculiar to the north. By the Spring Assize the trappers who were the witnesses had scattered to their far-flung traplines. As a consequence, it was October, 10 months after the crime, before Steve Poole heard himself pronounced guilty and given life imprisonment.

That ended the case insofar as justice was concerned. But where does Sergeant George Clark's cap fit into this northern saga? Well, it seems that on the rough return trip from Fort Ware, everyone was airsick. Because the plane was so crowded nobody could move. Bush planes didn't come equipped with little bags for such emergencies so the Sergeant faced a rapidly mounting crisis. The only quick solution was to use his cap. Wan and somewhat shaky when he stepped from the plane at McLeod Lake, he tossed the cap aside in disgust. Immediately, three hungry husky dogs leaped on it.

Before one could say "Welcome to McLeod Lake," they devoured it, peak and all. Well, not exactly all. George got the badge back.

The regulatory "period of wear" for a cap was one year. Unfortunately, George's was nearly new. As a result his requisition for a replacement was queried by the Quartermaster Stores in far off Victoria. They wanted an explanation.

Now George had more than normal proficiency with the written word. Drawing on his knowledge of the north, as a hobby he contributed quite a few articles to Britain's *Boys' Own Paper.*

So, seating himself at the typewriter, he gave Headquarters bureaucrats the explanation. "On March 3rd, 1943," he started, "as the party which had been holding an inquest at Fort Ware was about to embark on the plane at that point, Mr. Copeland, the manager of the Hudson's Bay post, called us in to lunch consisting of roast beef, potatoes, carrots, peas and rhubarb pie."

At this point his superiors in Victoria must have wondered why all this detail about a meal now almost a year old. But there was a reason, as was later evident.

George made particular mention of the seating arrangement in the over-crowded plane, everyone crammed in "with knees intertwined." Then the flight got rough. "About this time," he reports, "we were circling for a landing at the Forks and the plane was tossed about like a leaf in violent wind gusts.... We circled, jumped, side slipped, zoomed and finally dropped into an air pocket to a point so low we could almost touch the trees."

"The pilot decided he couldn't land without a fair chance of cracking up. I had been scared we were going to crash ... by now I was afraid we wouldn't!"

He went on to describe how Constable Russell "was beginning to have trouble controlling his eyes which had commenced to roll up a little," and how "the Indian prisoner had become so frightened he was weeping.

"By this time," continued George "Bill Harris, who had been looking sicker and sicker and had been hanging on to himself until we landed at Finlay Forks, finally felt further procrastination impossible. He clapped his gloved hands to his face and his body gave a convulsive heave."

The result was immediate and disastrous "...and he appeared for a moment to be crying rhubarb pie!"

He then described his own discomfort and how, in the absence of a proper receptacle, he had to substitute his cap. And added how they rocketed into McLeod Lake for a landing where he tossed aside his loaded cap in disgust. The dogs, he said, "thought that Santa Claus had arrived."

The report concluded with the time-honored "...in view of the above may I be supplied with a new cap ... size 6⅞?"

For Sergeant Clark, the Fort Ware episode wasn't all
negative. Although he did lose his uniform cap and
was marooned by the blizzard, during the latter
confinement he learned first-hand from
trapper Mort Teare about the

Murder Of A Special Constable

by Sergeant G. H. Clark

During 1907 Mort Teare and his brother, Henry, had been engaged
in buying horses around Kamloops and driving them up the trails
along the North Thompson River as far as Blue River, then north to
Yellowhead Pass. Yellowhead at this time was the scene of much
activity, as it was a base for construction camps of the Grand Trunk
Pacific Railway being built across Central B.C. from Eastern Canada to a new Pacific Ocean port called Prince Rupert. Horses, particularly pack animals, were in great demand by engineers and
surveyors.

Shortly after leaving Yellowhead in October on the return trip
to Kamloops, the Teares were overtaken and joined by a man riding a buckskin horse, and followed by a Hambletonian bay and a
two-year-old colt. The stranger gave his name as Williams and said
he came from Alberta. He was a man of middle age, short and
slightly built. He had light hair and a sandy complexion. What impressed the Teares was the dead-pan expression on his face,

The construction camp at Tete Jaune Cache where Mort and Henry Teare
delivered their horses and were later joined by Williams. The white tent at
center is a combination poolhall-barber shop.

heightened by cold grey eyes which stared arrogantly at the world in general.

The newcomer volunteered little information regarding himself, but did say that he had been in the South African War, and was heading for the Bulkley Valley in Northwestern British Columbia. Williams carried a 32.40 Savage rifle and a .22 rifle. On a belt strapped around his waist was a .445 Webley revolver in a holster. The others noticed that Williams invariably placed this revolver beneath his pillow when he lay down at night. He seemed to be well supplied with ammunition as he was constantly shooting at objects as he rode along.

The three men travelled on together and between Tete Jaune Cache and Blue River the buckskin horse got stuck in a mud hole. Without the slightest hesitation Williams dismounted and in the most cold-blooded manner drew his hunting knife and cut its throat. This action amazed the Teares. In a country where horses were highly valued, they could see no reason for such senseless cruelty.

Near Thunder River the party met an engineer accompanied by an Indian, and they stopped to talk. The engineer told them he had left caches at Blue River and at Hells Gate on the North Thompson River, and the Indian said he had left two horses at Blue River as one had gone lame.

On arriving at Blue River, Williams wanted to take oats from the Indian's cache but was dissuaded by the Teares. Caches were held inviolate by the unwritten law of the wilds. No decent man touched another's cache unless forced by dire necessity.

During the next day the Teares decided they had had enough of Williams. In the evening when they camped they suggested to their unwelcome companion that he travel alone. They told him how to reach Little Fort where there was a ferry which would take him across the river to the foot of the Cariboo Trail.

Shortly afterward the Indian left the engineer and returned to Blue River for his horses, only to discover that the good one had gone. Figuring it had been stolen, he built a raft and started down the North Thompson River in pursuit. Near Hells Gate he passed Williams riding along the trail beside the river. The Indian recognized the horse that Williams was riding as the one for which he was looking. Reaching the rapids some miles further downstream he abandoned the raft and hastened to Chu Chua where he reported the theft to Magistrate William Fennell.

In the meantime, Williams continued down the trail. When he reached the settlement of Vavenby he ransacked the cabin of Frank Allingham who returned home shortly afterwards and sent an Indian with a letter to Magistrate Fennell.

At Little Fort, an abandoned Hudson's Bay Trading Post five

miles north of Chu Chua, lived Bob Williams with his family. He was the ferryman at Little Fort and a Special Constable who served when needed.

When Magistrate Fennell received the Indian's complaint and Allingham's letter, he issued a warrant for the arrest of the horse thief. He sent it by the Indian to Bob Williams with instructions to arrest the thief when he came along. Soon the horse thief rode up. The Constable had put his revolver in his pocket and went to meet the man who dismounted by the ferry. After some questioning the Officer decided that Williams was the man he was looking for, and informed him he was under arrest. Mrs. Williams from a window in her home watched her husband approach the stranger and talk with him. Suddenly, she saw both men draw revolvers. There was a sharp report, her husband staggered and fell to the ground. He immediately struggled to his feet and stumbled towards the house. Before he had travelled 40 yards he pitched forward.

Mrs. Williams rushed to aid her husband, found he was beyond help and sent word to the Provincial Police at Kamloops 60 miles away. The murderer did not appear to be unduly excited. He returned to his horse, mounted and trotted off down the trail without making any attempt to cross the river. A later examination of the Special Constable's revolver showed that the firing mechanism was defective.

The Provincial Police at Kamloops was in charge of Chief Constable W. L. Fernie. It was to him that an exhausted Indian rushed, after riding all day and all night, with a tale in broken English of how Bob Williams "was no more." The Chief Constable informed the Coroner, and hastily gathered a group of men to act as a Coroner's Jury and Special Constables. A murder verdict was returned against the desperado. The body of Special Constable Bob Williams was buried, and the search for his slayer commenced.

All available men were sworn in as Special Constables for the posse, and word sent to all the Indians in the neighborhood to be on the look-out. Chief Constable Fernie was a great believer in the tracking ability of Indians. They liked him, and his confidence was rarely misplaced.

On a sand bar south of Little Fort foot prints were seen, which indicated that Williams had left his horse and taken to foot. The country between Little Fort and Chu Chua was scoured without success. Fernie decided that their quarry would be still trying to escape to the south. With the Chief Constable were three men — brothers Charlie and Duncan McLean, and Donald Gordon. These men were expert woodsmen and deadly shots. After a week of intensive searching, the posse had found no sign of the fugitive. When they reached Magistrate Fennell's house Fernie turned in for a decent rest in bed instead of on the ground.

In the middle of the night he was awakened by Fennell and told that an Indian woman had reported that she had seen a stranger about three miles down the river while she was getting water. It was dark, but as she dipped the bucket in the stream she saw a dug-out with the outline of a man in it drift silently past. She had heard of the search and hastened to Fennell with her news.

Chief Constable Fernie dressed hastily and with two men rode their tired horses to a point several miles below where the man had been seen in the canoe. They watched until dawn but saw nothing. Fernie then decided to return to Kamloops and start another posse working north from there. Leaving the search in charge of Charlie McLean, he hastened to Kamloops where he worked all day organizing another party. The following morning, just as they were about to leave, Charlie McLean rushed up, "I am very sorry, but we had to take him dead!".

He went on to explain that he and his brother, Duncan, with Donald Gordon, had called in at their home 20 miles north of Kamloops. Here they learned that a man had recently been seen walking along the road by the river.

McLean and Gordon took a short cut across some fields, and at a narrow place where the road was hemmed by dense underbrush concealed themselves and waited. They had not been in ambush long when they saw the fugitive approaching on foot. When opposite them, they stepped from their hiding place and accosted him, ordering him to hand over his rifle. With one hand Williams proffered the rifle. At the same time he reached with the other for his revolver, exclaiming, "I have another gun here!"

He fired at the two Specials, but drowning the explosion of the .455 was the sharp crack of the two Winchesters. The bandit crumpled with one bullet through his heart, another through his throat.

At the inquest which followed McLean and Gordon were absolved from all blame, having only done their duty as Constables.

On Williams' body was a money belt which contained $500 in U.S. $20 gold pieces. Papers showed that his name was H. C. Williams, but that he had used an alias of Anderson. On tracing the bandit's record, the police established that he was a U.S. citizen, known in law enforcement circles south of the border as a horse thief.

He wasn't the first — or the last — U.S. desperado to flee north in the mistaken belief that B.C. was a lawless land — and too late realize their error.

Citizens were occasionally sworn into the B.C.
Provincial Police as Special Constables. One of them
was a gruff loner who loved the wilderness, rum and
his herd of 200 horses. He was

John "Skook" Davidson — A Northern Legend

by Daryl Drew

Of all the legends that abound in the Canadian West, the stories
about Special Constable, horse packer and rancher Skook Davidson
rank high. One of Canada's most colorful pioneers, his character
and independence made many memorable campfire yarns.

Skook, whose real name was John Ogalvie Davidson, was
born in Scotland in 1892. His family was large and he was a bit
on the wild side as a youngster. As a consequence, he was
shipped to Canada at 13. Years later he acquired the nickname
"Skook" which remained with him all his life. It was from a chinook
word "Skookum," meaning strong, bestowed because of his
personal strength and the fact that he faced most problems like a
grizzly bear, head on.

On one adventure he led a mile-long pack train of 22
horses over a 500-mile trail. Skook had no help and each horse
carried about 200 pounds. Despite the fact he had to unload
the horses, pack them and wrangle them himself for the two-
week trip, Skook amazingly arrived on schedule.

On another occasion while crossing the Findlay River close
to the rapids, Skook went missing for a day and his crew as-
sumed that he had drowned. He had gotten into fast water but
kept hold of his horse's tail and emerged a few miles downstream. He was not pleased with the unseasonal bath but it was
typical of Skook's ability to survive a serious accident.

Skook was a mix of good-hearted generosity, gruff individu-
alism and wild independence. His loud voice, bellowing his
favorite saying to his horses, "Come on, ya heathen mavericks,"
could be heard long before the bells of his packstring. Everyone
knew when Skook was coming down the trail. A continuous
practical joker, he also had his serious side and once his temper
was aroused Skook didn't hesitate to settle matters with a brawl.

Skook learned his packing skills from B.C.'s legendary Jean
"Cataline" Caux, one of North America's finest packers. Skook's
apprenticeship with Cataline, however, ended over a disagree-
ment about a girl. Cataline showed his displeasure by laying a

Skook on his favorite horse, Poison, at his remote, mountain-flanked Diamond J Ranch. Access was by pack trail or float plane.

knife blade across Skook's throat. Davidson left to work for himself.

He bought an eight-horse team and planned to take up freighting. But by then World War One had broken out, an adventure that Skook could not resist. He sold his team in Ashcroft, went on a week long "whoop up" and joined the Canadian Mounted Rifles. He served in France as a scout, was wounded and generally saw enough action to dent his craving for adventure. His friends called Skook the most promoted soldier in the war. He made Sergeant 17 times, but always managed to get demoted. When the war ended he had risen back to Corporal, his decorations for bravery including the Distinguished Conduct Medal and Bar, the Military Medal and the French Croix de Guerre.

In 1920 he moved to Fort St. James and partnered with another packer named Earl Buck. They started a freight wagon business to the gold camps around Manson Creek and Germanson Landing. In addition, the B.C. Government was beginning to survey the northern portion of the province and Skook made extra money packing for surveyors, as well as supplying mining camps. On one occasion in 1920 Skook visited Esquimalt near Victoria. While enjoying a beer in a local pub six American sailors got a little loud about "How the Yanks won the war." Skook's blue eyes flashed and he jumped onto the sailors' table, yelling, "Well, here's one damn war ya won't win." He began brawling with all six, and it took an equal number of policemen to cart the frontiersman off to jail. He was released after promising to be on the next boat and not return to Esquimalt. The banishment suited the wilderness loving Skook just fine.

Offsetting Skook's somewhat rowdy disposition was his reliability. Even with temperature at -60°F he delivered much needed supplies to the mining camps. When roads were built to the mines in the 1940s and the region became too "civilized," Skook said goodbye to the Fort St. James area and headed north to homestead in the isolated Kechika Valley.

He had first seen the valley in 1939, knew it was in a snow shadow and decided to start his famous Diamond J Ranch at the foot of Terminus Mountain. He lived alone in this isolation except for a visit by an occasional trapper or prospector, or when he hired packers or game guides. An eternal practical joker, Skook used to play a trick on his guides he called the "Diamond J haircut." It left the victim practically bald to return home after a season in the bush. Skook insisted it was a good test to see if the victim's girl friend really loved him.

Skook's great pride was his horse herd of some 200 head. He was very particular about how they were cared for. Old animals were pensioned off around the ranch instead of being shot as was the northern custom. When Skook gave a tour to one visitor he spoke nostalgically about horses that had died of old age. At a pile of aging bones he paused and said, "That's Belle. She was 30 when she died and a good horse, too."

In 1964 his favorite saddle horse, Poison, came up lame and had to be put down. The horse had been gentle with Skook, but would kick anyone else who came near. Skook was heartbroken when he had to shoot Poison after they had shared 17 years on the trails.

With so many horses in so isolated an area, one of Skook's problems was preventing in-breeding. He preferred to use draft-horse studs because their offspring were stout enough to carry heavy loads long distances and big enough to keep the loads dry while crossing rivers.

Skook knew each of his 200 horses by name and in 1969 spent $1,000 a month flying in feed when the snow got deep. He had no tolerance for anyone who mistreated his animals. One wrangler who worked briefly for Skook left the horses tied up to trees after reaching camp because he had hurt his arm. A furious Skook demanded to know why the horses were still loaded. After the wrangler explained about his arm Skook dropped him with a punch to the jaw, bellowing that he didn't care how hurt he was, the horses came first.

He was apparently equally forthright after being bothered by horse thieves. Although he would not give details he did mention that some rustlers had never left his valley, the basis for stories that there were more than old horse bones buried along the Kechika River.

Davidson would often leave on pack trips in May and return to the Diamond J in November. He celebrated a successful trip with a bottle of overproof rum because he said Scotch had no kick. He would arrive in camp and toss a half empty bottle to someone. If questioned why there was any left he would say, "Will power, my boy, will power. Of course I started out with a couple of dozen bottles."

Until the Alaska Highway was built, Skook brought his supplies into the ranch over the arduous trails of Sifton Pass from Fort Ware some 120 roadless miles to the south. He would also get supplies from Lower Post near the Yukon border. He was known for descending on Lower Post and treating the settlement to a two-day party. Skook's Landing on the route is named after him.

In 1940 he was given the rank of Special Constable in the B.C. Provincial Police Force because of his knowledge of the north country. Part of his duties was acting as Coroner. While officiating at an old trapper's burial he reverently removed his black stetson and said, "Thank God it's you Pete and not me. Cover him up boys." Skook was never one for long ceremonies.

When helicopters put horse packers out of the exploration business, Skook switched to big-game guiding. He was an ardent conservationist and hated hunting but the revenue permitted him to stay on his ranch. He was as concerned about surrounding wildlife as he was about his horses. None of his clients — and some were very wealthy and influential — were permitted to indiscriminately kill any animal. His guiding area covered 5,000 square miles on both sides of the Kechika River, the Diamond J as base camp. An average hunting trip covered 300 miles and he once guided for the Shah of Iran's brother, Prince Abdarreza. He bellowed at him the same as anyone else. At the end of the trip the Prince presented him with a silver bowl because Skook was the first man to treat him like a real person.

The Diamond J Ranch consisted of a half dozen log buildings, some corrals, miles of fences and a network of trails. It was named after the famous diamond hitch used to tie packs onto horses and mules, and the J from Skook's first name.

Life at the Diamond J was spartan — very spartan. During his first winter he survived until spring on 25 pounds of flour, fresh game meat, 10 pounds of sugar and one pound of tea and coffee. The toilet was outdoors, of course, the cabin roofs were dirt and bathing for the most part was in the creek. But to Skook it was home and suited him just fine. He was, in some ways, a mix of opposing traits. While he would growl at anyone using too much canned milk or sugar — "Coffee was made to be swallowed black," — he always helped people he could.

During the winter of 1965, for instance, temperature in the Kechika Valley plummeted to -54°F. Some miles from Skook's ranch on the Turnagain River Joseph Hayes and his wife, Emma, were caring for a game guide's horses. In early January two of their children — 5-year-old George and 15-month-old Gloria — were sick with pneumonia. Surrounded by total wilderness, the pair didn't even have a dog team to help them. There only hope, they decided, was to snowshoe to Skook's ranch where there was a radiotelephone. In the sub-zero cold they set out, Joseph carrying Gloria and packing George on his shoulders. Emma struggled along with their other child, a 6-month-old boy. They had no tent, a bush shelter their only protection. After three terrible days Gloria died. Hayes made a cache for her in a tree.

The next afternoon her brother died and his body was also cached in a tree. By now Emma was exhausted and Hayes headed for trapper Louis Boya's cabin on the Kechika where he could leave Emma and his surviving infant son.

They reached the cabin cold, hungry and exhausted. Nevertheless, Hayes left to struggle four more days to Skook's, freezing his foot along the way. A plane was summoned and landed on the frozen Kechika River near Boya's cabin. The bodies of the dead children were later carried to Watson Lake some 150 miles by two friends of the Hayes family.

Two years previously Skook had unknowingly saved the lives of two people. A plane heading for Seattle from Alaska with pilot Ralph Flores and passenger Helen Klaben had crashed about 50 miles northwest of where the Hayes family lost their two children. Flores and Klaben spent 49 days without food until pilot Chuck Hamilton saw an SOS in the snow while taking supplies and guide Jack George to Skook's ranch. They landed at a lake near Louis Boya's cabin and the pair were saved.

Since disaster can strike quickly in the northern isolation, with no help for miles, it is amazing that Skook survived his years of living alone. Finally, however, even his rugged constitution fell prey to time. Arthritis set into his hips and it became increasingly difficult for him to live in his beloved wilderness. After a bad fire at the ranch in 1972 and the tragic death of his friend and cook, Mabel Frank, he was eventually taken to a resthome in Vancouver. Here Special Constable Skook Davidson died at 86.

A poem he wrote at the Diamond J in 1949 sums up his philosophy. He called it, appropriately,

AN ODE TO THE NORTH
Tis time to live, when all the north
Without a fence or fuss,
Belongs in partnership with God,
The government and us.

When our souls sing peace and rest,

Beyond the Great Divide,
Just put us on some stretch of North
That is sunny, lone and wide.

A skyline fence from East to West
With room to go and come,
We liked our fellow man the best
When he was scattered some.

The wolves may rob our headstones now,
And coyotes call their kin;
While horses come and paw the mounds,
But don't you fence us in.

Prosecuting a dangerous driver, catching a car thief,
settling a domestic quarrel and performing a
wedding were all part of a policeman's duty during

A Day On Detachment

Typical of officers in rural Detachments was
Constable Robert Ross who spent over 10
years at Shawnigan Lake near Duncan. Like
Constables Kelly and de Goutiere, his duties
were extremely varied.

"10 a.m. To office and to Duncan re Court."

As Constable Kelly scrawled the notation in the Chemainus Detachment Daily Diary, he idly wondered what variety of work the day might hold. It was a Saturday in September 1948, starting just like many another day at the beginning of the hunting season.

Nearby, Constable Justin de Goutiere was busily issuing firearms licences and deer tags to several residents. One man fidgeting nervously with an envelope in his hands appeared to have something else on his mind. Enquiry revealed that he wished to register a new-born son and heir to his worldly goods. After quickly scanning the forms to check for possible errors, Kelly procured a birth certificate, typed out the details, signed it and sent the new father on his way to the Post Office to obtain family allowance forms.

He gathered up a sheaf of blue papers and advised Constable de Goutiere of his expected time of return, then headed for Duncan in the Detachment police car. The trip was uneventful, apart from checking a motorist exceeding the speed limit at the Chemainus River Bridge, and Kelly enjoyed the drive in the cool autumn sunshine.

After successful prosecution of a dangerous driving charge before the Magistrate's court, Kelly made returns of various monies collected by both the North Cowichan Municipal and Provincial Government offices and again headed back to Chemainus. Stops were made enroute to serve two Civil Court Summonses and take details of a complaint involving theft of tools from a small sawmill.

At the Chemainus office, Constable de Goutiere was just finishing off a crime report as Kelly walked in. "Don't forget your wedding this afternoon, Reverend Kelly," de Goutiere quipped. "The bridegroom phoned twice this morning to enquire about the time."

"Son-of-a-gun," said Kelly. "That's right, they're coming at 2:30 and it's 1:00 o'clock now. Let's eat and then there will just be time to clean up the courtroom and rehearse my lines before they arrive."

At 2:30 p.m., after replacing his tunic and Sam Browne with a dark suit coat, Kelly performed the civil marriage ceremony for a nervous young couple of different religions who had decided the civil ceremony provided the proper compromise in this regard. The ceremony was simple, but dignified, the bride tearful, but happy. The legality of the marriage was quickly made even more binding by its immediate registration by Kelly in his dual role of Marriage Commissioner and District Registrar of births, deaths and marriages.

The wedding over, de Goutiere and Kelly closed the office for a while. They then patrolled Chemainus town and the highway area, watching for speeders and offenders against traffic and other statutes, stopping also at a local residence to secure a short statement from a witness in a pending Assize Court case. After refuelling the police car for the week-end ahead, both men returned to the office and checked out for supper, but not before three more hunting licences and a driver's licence had been issued to local residents.

Returning to the office at 8:00 p.m., Constable Kelly spent the next hour or so writing up various complaints in the office offence book, then began patrolling the town and highway area about Chemainus. There was considerable traffic on the roads and the local licenced premises were crowded as usual on a Saturday evening. Nothing unusual occurred until 10:20 p.m. Kelly was checking through the Horseshoe Bay Inn when he was approached by an excited resident who stated his car had been stolen from in front of the Inn sometime since 9:00 p.m. During this time the owner had been in the beer parlor and had left the car parked at the roadside, unlocked and with ignition keys in it. He had purchased the car very recently and did not know the licence number. The other details were quickly telephoned to Duncan and Ladysmith Detachments for furtherance to Victoria, Nanaimo and other Vancouver Island Detachments.

Taking the stranded owner with him, Kelly began a systematic check of the town and the highway northward for the stolen vehicle. He returned to the Detachment office to check for calls before resuming the search south of town. Here he was advised by Mrs. Kelly that a bad accident had been reported about two miles south of town.

"Sounds like your stolen car," was Kelly's only comment to the startled owner as the police car sped to the scene. And it was. The stolen car, a large 1938 model sedan, was completely blocking the highway. It was so badly smashed that it brought profane threats to the lips of the angry owner. Another car, a small roadster of ancient vintage, was lying by the side of the road, the left front wheel and side broken and smashed.

Glass and pieces of torn metal littered the road, making it evident that the two cars had struck at high speed. A crowd of spectators and cars were gathering quickly. After dispatching a young fellow to contact a wrecking truck to clear the highway, Kelly located another youth, suffering from several cuts on his face, who readily admitted he had been driving the roadster. He stated the larger car had come over to his side of the road, travelling fast, and he had no chance to avoid the collision. His foot had been pinned under the dashboard, his eye-glasses broken and he was slightly stunned by the impact. By the time he recovered and climbed out of his vehicle, the driver of the other car had vanished. Other motorists were questioned, but apparently the driver of the stolen car had made his escape before anyone had arrived on the scene. It was obvious, however, that he must have received a few cuts and bruises.

For a while Kelly had his hands full controlling the traffic while the wrecker pulled the smashed vehicles off the roadway, and keeping the curious motorists moving on afterwards. The area surrounding the highway was heavily wooded. A quick search along the road revealed that the thief could have made his way into the woods at many points and was biding his time until the excitement died away. But he also may have walked along the highway immediately after the accident and secured a ride in either direction. Having no facilities for searching the extensive wooded area, Kelly decided to gamble that the culprit was hiding and would come out when he thought it safe.

An hour later, after driving the injured driver of the roadster to the hospital and checking the telephone office for calls, Kelly headed for the scene of the accident. Suddenly, his headlights picked up a man walking quickly towards town, keeping well to the left side of the road. As the police car stopped beside him the man raised his hand as if to cover his face. Kelly shone the flashlight on the walker. He noticed a bad cut over the man's left eye. Under questioning the man stated that he was a seaman turned logger, now employed at the local logging camp, that he had been drinking beer and liquor all day, and had got into a fight after visiting an acquaintance down the road, thus receiving the injury to his eye. Constable Kelly, however, noticed leaves and twigs clinging to the man's rough mackinaw shirt and felt that his replies were evasive. He asked the man to come to the police office and establish his identity. Further questioning left no doubt in Kelly's mind that he had the man responsible for the stolen and smashed car. After being arrested, warned and searched, he was placed in the lockup until morning.

The balance of the night was uneventful, with nothing more important to mark in the diary than warning to a local drunk and breaking up of a domestic quarrel.

"3:30 a.m. Premises checked. Town quiet and orderly. To residence."

Kelly yawned as he closed the diary and turned off the office lights.

P.S. — The prisoner admitted taking the car and was convicted.

Of all policeman's duties, none is more thankless
and dangerous than

Tracking Insane Killers

by Deputy Commissioner Cecil Clark

Humanity at its best is a frail thing. None know this fact better
than police whose files contain many stories of tragedies and heart-
aches. But of all tragedies, none is as sad as those when the mind
of man weakens. Nor is there a task more dangerous or thankless
than that faced by police when these dread reports reach their offices.

One of the most tragic is that of Cosens Spencer, wealthy
owner of the Chilco Ranch in the Chilcotin. On September 10, 1930,
Spencer suddenly went insane and seized a 16-gauge shotgun. Before anyone had grasped his intention he turned on two of his
employees, with whom he had been conversing, and fired two
shots. The first struck W. H. Stoddard in his right arm. The second
tore into Edward Smith's back, killing him instantly.

Spencer immediately vanished. The police were notified and
search was started.

But no trace of Spencer could be found. Mrs. Spencer offered a
reward of $2,000 but it brought no immediate results. The police,
acting purely on theory, felt that Spencer had committed suicide by
drowning himself in the Chilcotin River.

Nevertheless, an intensive hunt was organized. Every inch of
that wild country was combed by expert trackers. Meanwhile,

The Chilco Ranch house where Edward Smith was murdered.

Sergeant Gallagher and Little Charlie found Cosens Spencer's body in the Chilcotin River.

The Saari Ranch where John Lake suddenly started shooting at his fellow workers.

cranks flooded the police with hundreds of suggestions. Most of them were useless, but investigated and tried on the chance that something might prove of value. Nothing was learned.

Then on October 9, almost one month after the tragedy, an Indian found a body in the Chilcotin River. A little further upstream was a 16-gauge shotgun. The body was that of Cosens Spencer. The shotgun, too, was his.

Just why should a man of Spencer's position suddenly go berserk and kill a faithful employee? To this question we have no answer. It could be said that Spencer suffered somewhat from hallucinations, for in January 1927 he had charged a prominent rancher with killing one of his steers. At the subsequent trial the rancher was acquitted, but Spencer wasn't satisfied. He appealed the verdict and asked that the case be re-opened. It was, and again the accused was acquitted. It was proved that the man did kill a steer, but Spencer couldn't prove that the animal belonged to him.

Another case involving an animal killing south of the Chilco Ranch a few years later also resulted in the death of an innocent man. On October 3, 1932, Game Warden A. E. Farey came upon a party of three men about 26 miles up the North Fork of the Yalakom River. One of them was Frank Gott, an Indian who had an illegally shot fawn deer.

It was about 3 p.m. when Farey came upon the party. The animal had evidently just been shot. He asked to examine the hide, and in so doing turned his back on the party. Suddenly he heard Gott call out, "Stand to, Mr. Farey!"

Farey turned, but before he saw Gott, a bullet crashed into his back and killed him instantly. Farey slumped to the ground.

Gott's companions were horrified. They left at once to notify the police at Lillooet. Sergeant H. N. Wood took some Constables and hurried to the scene where they found Farey's body. A note in Gott's handwriting was pinned to Farey's clothing, "I am now going to commit suicide."

Sergeant Wood considered this note. He was not impressed by it. A man, he reasoned, who would shoot an unarmed man in the back lacked the moral courage to commit suicide. If, as the crime indicated, the man had suddenly gone mad, then it was not likely he would do away with himself until he had inflicted further damage on whoever chanced to aggravate him.

A search was instituted. It went on through the night, and next morning Sergeant Wood's theories about suicide were proven correct. Gott had called at a neighbor's place and, unknown to the neighbor, had slept in a barn. This informant, a cripple, said that Gott called at the house and demanded food. Aware of the shooting, the man had tried to detain Gott by promising to cook something. Gott refused to listen. He asked for food at once. On receiving it started for the woods.

"They'll never take me alive," he told this man. "I'll kill them before they see me."

Sergeant Wood at once realized that Gott had no set plan of escape. But he also realized that it would be useless to try and follow a man like Gott in that country. He knew every inch of it and could evade capture quite easily.

The Sergeant's knowledge of Gott's personality was not reassuring. He was known in the community as a hot-tempered man who seemed to be mentally unbalanced at times. He had served in the Great War as a sniper, and was a superb shot. Such a man, Sergeant Wood knew, was apt to prove dangerous. He called in more men.

If Gott knew the country, Sergeant Wood was also familiar with certain parts of it. He knew that Gott would have to cross the Yalakom River to secure food and arms from the Indians there. He had friends in the tribe who would shelter him and aid him in a siege. Such a situation must be avoided at all costs, the Sergeant decided. If Gott dug himself in on the reserve there would be loss of life before he was captured. In the interests of all concerned, Gott must be prevented from crossing.

Sergeant Wood detailed his men to guard every part of the river. If Gott was sighted, he ordered, he must be called on to stop and every reasonable effort made to apprehend him. But under no circumstances must he be permitted to gain the safety of the other side. If he did, lives were certain to be lost.

Sergeant Robertson of the Game Department and Game Warden Quesnel took up their posts near a small suspension bridge about three miles from the scene of the shooting. Throughout the long night hours they kept a close watch on the shores and on the bridge.

As dawn was breaking Gott suddenly appeared. He saw the officers waiting for him. Sergeant Robertson called on him to surrender. He refused, and immediately made a desperate dash for the river.

Sergeant Robertson remembered his orders. It was impossible to catch Gott, who was fleeing like a deer. But he must be stopped. A crack shot and also a World War veteran, Robertson took careful aim. He fired. Gott fell, a bullet in his leg. The two officers dashed to his side just in time to prevent him slashing his throat with a hunting knife.

In view of subsequent events it is important to remember that Sergeant Robertson was a crack shot. He could have shot Gott in the back of the head had he been so disposed. But, he put a bullet, not in the bone, but merely through the fleshy section of Gott's leg.

Gott, however, died. He did not die from the effects of the bullet wound but advanced tuberculosis. After he died critics raised a storm of protest at the methods used by the police. They ignored the fact that a dedicated Game Warden doing his duty, a married man with a splendid war record, had been shot in the back without a chance to defend himself. They chose to ignore the obvious truth that Gott was a dangerous man, ready to snuff out still more lives if he could have crossed the river. They brushed aside all facts and made a mockery of justice by heaping criticism on men who warranted the highest commendation.

But the unfortunate Farey wasn't the only Game Warden to be murdered. Two years previously in East Kootenay, Game Warden Dennis Greenwood had driven into the community of Canal Flats and stopped in front of the store.

Greenwood, his wife at his side, was seated in his car, chatting with one of the residents. Then William Edward Floyd came along the street. He saw Greenwood's car and called the officer. Suspecting nothing, Greenwood got out and accompanied Floyd to the rear of the car. Without the slightest warning, Floyd drew a revolver and shot the unfortunate officer dead.

The police were notified and Constable J. Kirkup, well knowing the temper of the man he was hunting, commenced a search. For all he knew, Floyd might shoot him from ambush. But he went nevertheless.

Later that day the Constable went to Floyd's house to conduct a closer search of the premises. He heard steps on the back porch. Throwing open the back door he came face to face with the wanted killer.

For a moment the two men faced each other. Finally, Floyd said, "I've come to give myself up."

Constable Kirkup placed him under arrest. On October 13, 1930, Floyd went on trial at the Fernie Assizes. He was committed to an insane asylum.

It seems incredible that men, apparently harmless one minute, can suddenly go mad and nothing but the taking of a life, no matter how innocent, will satisfy them. The pathetic case of John Lake is an example.

On August 26, 1935, Lake, who lived with the Saari family near Colleymount south of Burns Lake, lay in his bunk all day and would not speak to anyone. He had lived with the family for eight years, and though subject to fits of melancholia and extreme depression, was considered harmless. The family thought nothing of him staying in and went about their work.

About six o'clock, the day's work over, the men were unhitching the teams when Lake suddenly leaped from his bed, seized a .303 rifle and rushed outside. He saw Frank Saari and quickly fired a shot at him. It went through his cap but left him unharmed. Saari immediately dropped to the ground and crawled behind some bushes.

Lake next turned on Emil Perle. The frightened man asked Lake not to shoot. His answer was a soft-nose bullet which tore into the lower part of his abdomen. Perle dropped, mortally wounded.

August Kivi, another farm hand, saw what was about to be his fate. He dashed behind a farm building and escaped. For a moment Lake stood glaring around. Not seeing another victim he then ran into the bush. Saari, not daring to move for fear of drawing fire, waited in his hiding place. About 25 minutes later he heard a shot that seemed to be in the place where Lake disappeared. Saari, believing that Lake had committed suicide, left his cover and ran to notify the police.

Constable Sandy of the Burns Lake Detachment answered the call and left with a doctor. But Perle had died 10 minutes before they arrived. The Constable investigated the area pointed out by Saari, but could find no trace of either Lake or his body. He had simply vanished. His photograph was distributed on police circulars and a reward offered. Nothing was heard.

Police, and those who knew Lake, are certain he died. Saari is positive that he ran into the bush of the wild country and kept going until he fell and died of exhaustion. Since no news of him has appeared it is likely that somewhere in the bush lies the remains of another man whose mind weakened.

Fortunately, not all of these sad cases end in tragedy for the innocent. Take the case of Peter McCleese who lived with his mother and the House family at Ochiltree in the Cariboo. McCleese had acted peculiarly from time to time, but no serious view was taken of this actions.

However, he seemed to harbor a strong resentment towards a family named Rose who lived a short distance from the House residence.

On the morning of December 10, 1932, he suddenly took his rifle and said he was going out on his trapline. He might need his gun to shoot a coyote which had been robbing his traps.

Miss House, however, knew that McCleese harbored a fancied wrong against the Rose family. She saw him prepare to leave, saw him take his rifle. Something warned her that McCleese had suddenly gone insane. She saw him go to the barn and saddle a horse. Fearing what he would do she bravely went out to speak to him. He muttered something about "going to get them all" and galloped off in the direction of the Rose residence. Miss House, now certain that tragedy was about to strike, sent her brother Laurel over to warn her neighbors.

Louis James Carson was sawing wood outside the Rose home

when McCleese arrived. Before the unfortunate man knew what was taking place, McCleese unloosed a bullet which struck him in his right arm. The insane man suddenly turned and saw Mr. Rose standing near the house. He fired two shots at him. Laurel House arrived at this moment, and McCleese fired at him. House and Rose dashed for the shelter of the home. McCleese fired another shot then galloped away.

Such was the state of McCleese's mind that he imagined he had killed everyone he had fired at. He returned to the House home where he told Miss House that he had cleaned up the Rose family. He put the horse away and then told Miss House that he was going to shoot himself. He went down the trail towards the barn and Miss House ran into her home for help. She had scarcely got inside when she heard a shot from somewhere near the barn. A man nearby, who had also heard the shot, ran to the house and was told what had taken place. He immediately went down the trail to the place where he had heard the shot and there he found Peter McCleese with the top of his head blown off.

Constable S. E. Raybone investigated this case. He saw the body of the unfortunate man lying beside the trail that led to House's barn. The rifle was held between the arms and legs and suicide was evident.

In the unfortunate McCleese case there was little danger to the Constable responding to the call. But circumstances were totally different in a case involving a man named Mansfield who became obsessed with the idea that he was being discriminated against by a government road-building party.

Mansfield, an intermittently belligerent person, took a strong dislike to Mr. Whiting, the foreman of the gang which was working on a road just out of Natal in the East Kootenay. Though his subsequent actions indicated that he was bordering on insanity, Mansfield retained sufficient mental balance to warrant being classified as sane so far as the law was concerned. However, he speedily proved that sane or not he was a dangerous person who would stop at nothing.

On the evening of August 19, 1925, Mansfield left his home and approached the members of the road gang. He ordered them to stop work. Somewhat surprised, and then amused, the men laughed at him and went on with their duties. Furious, Mansfield returned home and got his rifle. His mental control fled. Racing back to where the gang were working, he opened fire without warning. Two men fell, wounded. Mansfield, yelling defiance, ran into the bush.

The police were notified and Sergeant G. H. Greenwood, Constables A. J. Smith, F. Brindley, I. J. Brown and Probationer Ward set out at once. Darkness made locating the man difficult. It was evident that he was hiding in the woods, and it would be necessary to await daylight before anything could be done.

But daylight brought no news of Mansfield. The police began a systematic hunt for him, unaware that another grim tragedy was in the making. Mansfield was lying in ambush.

Foreman Whiting was returning to his home in Natal when he saw Mansfield step out on the road. Whiting had no option but to stop his car. It was a fatal move. Mansfield's murderous rifle cracked and Whiting was killed. Once again he fled to the bush.

Sergeant Greenwood took immediate steps to prevent a repetition of tragedy. Until now it had been thought that Mansfield, having shot three men, might realize the enormity of his crimes. Now, it appeared, the shootings had only increased his desire for more bloodshed. Sergeant Greenwood and his men intensified their efforts to apprehend the obviously insane killer.

The Sergeant detailed his men. Constable Smith was picked to watch Mansfield's home. The following evening, Smith saw Mansfield approaching the house. The officer did not draw his gun. Instead he walked straight up to the killer.

Mansfield's eyes gleamed. He was ready to kill once more. But he was now dealing with a cool, determined man who knew his duty and was prepared to carry it out regardless of the implied threats. Before he had a chance to bring his weapon into action, Mansfield was disarmed and placed under arrest.

Constable Smith's courageous action earned him high praise from police officials. Sergeant Greenwood and the other Constables were also mentioned for their good work in bringing this case to a successful end. To the policemen, however, it was part of their duty, although all were well aware that death could have awaited them.

In fact, in the Peace River Country in 1931, Constable A. J. Pomeroy was incredibly lucky that death passed him by. On May 24 at Fort St. John he was informed by Constable H. L. Norman of the Rolla Detachment that a man named Bryan had broken into a cabin and stolen a number of articles. The man, the report said, had left Fort St. John a day or so previous in company with another man who was driving a team. They were headed towards Halfway River. It was further added that the wanted man's name was Robert F. Stewart.

Constable Pomeroy saddled his horse and set off in pursuit. About 25 miles up the Halfway River he located the team and wagon. The driver and Stewart had just made camp. Pomeroy went forward to make the arrest.

Stewart saw him coming. He turned towards the wagon and said, "Just a minute," Pomeroy halted. Stewart suddenly about faced, .32 calibre revolver in his hand. He fired point blank at the

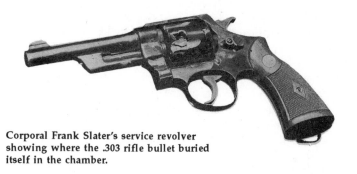

Corporal Frank Slater's service revolver
showing where the .303 rifle bullet buried
itself in the chamber.

Constable but missed. He tried another shot and Pomeroy jumped aside. Murder was in Stewart's eyes, the means in his hand.

The revolver flamed again and a bullet nicked Pomeroy's left ear. The Constable, having no other option, drew his revolver and returned the fire.

At the first shot the wanted man doubled up and ran away. Pomeroy followed. Running in a crouching position, Stewart turned quickly and fired two more shots at the Constable. Both missed the officer but smashed into the wagon behind. Stewart then ran into the bush and vanished. A quick search failed to discover him.

Constable Pomeroy decided it would be better to return to Fort St. John and get assistance before taking any more risks. A search party went out and combed the area but didn't find any trace of the man. Still, Constable Pomeroy was certain he had hit him.

Five months later a party of men found the remains of a body in the bush which was later identified as that of Stewart. He had died from the wound inflicted by the Constable during the fight. But it would have been Constable Pomeroy who died if the would-be killer's aim had been better.

In another instance of police versus the deranged, an officer's revolver saved his life. Not, however, because he fired it but because it deflected a rifle bullet that would likely have killed him. The drama was related in the *Shoulder Strap*, the Force's official magazine.

It began in August 1945 when Corporal Frank Slater and Constable Cyril N. Lee left Kimberley to investigate reports that an elderly rancher named Charles Bechtel who lived alone had been threatening neighbors with a double-bitted axe. When the officers arrived, Bechtel refused to open the door and threatened to shoot. The policemen returned to Kimberley and on August 21, Corporal Slater and Constables Lee and Pringle resumed their attempt to get Bechtel out of his cabin. This time they were armed with tear gas. After a vain parley through the locked door, Constable Lee fired a gas shell through a window. Bechtel fled to the brush armed with a .303 rifle. The police officers searched till dark when Constable Lee was despatched to notify district Sergeant W. J. McKay of the occurrence.

About 8:25 p.m. the watching officers spotted Bechtel who had circled to his cabin and entered. It was too risky to rush him in the dark but he could be heard coughing and moving in the cabin's dark interior. They maintained a watch all night and next morning, joined by Constable W. C. McLauchlin, the police squad noticed the cabin door ajar, but the door of a nearby cow barn closed. Corporal Slater, checking the barn through a window, saw Bechtel lying asleep. But as Sergeant McKay and Slater turned to make for the cow barn door two shots rang out. One narrowly missed the Sergeant, the other struck Corporal Slater's service revolver holstered on his belt. The concussion fired the revolver shell, the bullet striking Slater in the leg. Constable Lee fired gas shells into the barn and the police took cover to await results.

The cow barn was in a clearing and gave Bechtel good visibility in all directions. Bechtel was seen at the door, and during the morning 12 projectiles and four grenades were lobbed into the log building. Altogether about 35 shots were exchanged between the police and the besieged madman. As darkness fell, Bechtel was seen again in the doorway, this time obviously in distress. Corporal Moyer MacBrayne tried to persuade him to throw his gun away, but without success.

Next morning Sergeant McKay decided to do nothing except keep the barn surrounded. He knew they could take the old rancher as soon as his ammunition was exhausted.

About 12:30 p.m. the watchers were rewarded by seeing Bechtel walk unsteadily from the barn to his house, unarmed. He was immediately rushed and searched. Ill and suffering from a rifle wound in the hip, he was made as comfortable as possible and rushed by ambulance to the Kimberley hospital. Malnutrition complicated his condition, however, and he died the next day.

Sergeant McKay and his men were lucky in only having one slight casualty in their party. Their calm and steady handling of a difficult situation brought praise from both Commissioner Parsons and their Divisional Commander.

These are only a few of the potentially dangerous insanity cases handled by B.C. policemen. They are, however, representative of the work done by these gallant but unassuming men while serving British Columbians for almost a century.

Over the paved Alaska Highway, Fort Nelson is an easy five-hour drive from Fort St. John, a contrast to the 49 days two B.C. Provincial Policemen fought to

Blaze The Fort Nelson Trail

by Ronald White

Many stories have been written of the danger and hardships encountered by B.C. Provincial Policemen while upholding the law, stories which are part of the Province's colorful history. But in addition to maintaining the law, policemen performed a multitude of other duties.

Particularly in the northern sections, Police Officers were the sole agent of the Provincial Government. In many cases, they assisted considerably in opening up the north country. One of them was Inspector C. G. Barber. In fact there was probably no man on the entire Force who saw more of British Columbia.

Despite any claims to the contrary, for instance, Inspector Barber was the first man to traverse the miles of wilderness between Fort St. John and Fort Nelson, the route largely followed by today's Alaska Highway. Although trappers and prospectors had for years travelled the waterways in and out of Fort St. John and Fort Nelson, no cross-country connection had been established between the two posts. Supplies for Fort Nelson arrived via Great Slave Lake to Fort Smith, then up the Liard River.

Inspector Barber joined the Provincial Police on April 1, 1912, as a Special Constable. His first posting was to Lytton where he took part in the search for murderers Moses Paul and Paul Spentlum. (See *B.C. Provincial Police Stories: Volume One*.) He then served in a number of B.C. communities, including, from 1920 to 1929, Pouce Coupe, Fort St. John and Fort Nelson.

During the first years of his administration at Fort St. John, Constable Barber often wondered what lay over the divide in the country between Fort St. John and Fort Nelson, and wished he could make the trip through.

Then in August 1923, he received instructions from headquarters at Victoria to contact Constable E. Forfar at Hudson Hope and make a patrol to Fort Nelson, over 300 miles away through unknown wilderness.

Constable Barber's instructions were to take saddle and packhorses as far as possible, then build a raft and float down the Nelson River. Owing to the probability of having to leave the horses somewhere along the route, it was necessary to take a man to look after them.

Constables Barber and Forfar at the mouth of the Conroy River.

There were several purposes behind the patrol. The district was the last virgin game country in British Columbia and Indian and white trappers were gradually extending their operations. A large number of furs were finding their way into the Northwest Territories with the consequent considerable loss in fur royalties to British Columbia. It was therefore a part of his duties to ascertain as far as possible the number of white and Indian trappers, to check the quantity of furs going to the Northwest Territories, and to scan the books of the fur trading company at Fort Nelson for the preceding four years.

Moreover, the patrol called for a general survey of the country from an agricultural point of view, with further reports on the timber and mineral potential. Then, to make sure there were no idle moments, he was to make inquiries about two white trappers who had gone into the country the previous year. They had never been heard of again.

Once on the trail the men quickly discovered that a major problem was horse feed. It was so scarce in many areas that it often meant a trip of several miles in the morning to round up the horses. Although hobbled, they wandered during the night in search of food — always in the direction of home.

Travelling mostly by compass, the party spent 20 gruelling days cutting trail, pulling the horses out of muskeg where they got mired up to their bellies, and battling pestiferous hordes of black flies and no-see-ums. By now, the horses were exhausted from the insects, lack of feed and sore feet, the latter brought on by following creek and river beds as much as possible to save cutting trail through the brush and forest.

Near the mouth of the Conroy River beavers had built dams and flooded a considerable acreage of land. Meadows had formed and these now furnished ample horse feed. Since it was evident that they could not continue to Fort Nelson, the horses were made to swim the river and left in the meadows in charge of the extra man. He was given the major portion of the supplies, and plenty of pine tar and lard with which to smear the horses every morning. The flies were so bad the animals could not have been kept there until their return without this treatment.

They established a camp and began building a raft. Since a raft is cumbersome and unresponsive, it is a particularly dangerous method of transportation on an unknown river. Fortunately, they never had to use it.

Their campfire attracted the attention of Indians camped upriver and they came to investigate. These Indians had never before seen horses and it was some time before they were fully satisfied that they were harmless. Being cordially treated, they reciprocated and offered the two Constables a canoe made of spruce bark reinforced with split-willow ribs. Although the canoe would be much more manoeuvrable than the raft, it was still a hazardous means of travel. Had Constable Forfar not been a good canoeman, using the Indian craft would probably have been more suicidal than attempting the trip on their raft.

Ignoring the potential hazards, they loaded their equipment on the flimsy craft and cast off into the unknown waters of the Conroy, then the Nelson River. In four days they covered the 150 miles to Fort Nelson.

After two days attending to business they started back. But fighting upstream was a brutal contrast from gliding down. Because Constable Forfar was the more experienced canoeman and steered the craft, Constable Barber found himself on the end of a 100-foot trackline, pulling and poling the canoe upstream — for an obvious reason called "climbing the spruce pole." Icy baths were an unwelcome accompaniment. In contrast to the two-day downstream trip, they were 14 days fighting upstream to their horses. Here they rested two days before leaving on the 200-mile overland portion of the return trip.

Before this patrol was undertaken, a representative of the Provincial Government had suggested to Constable Barber that Constables stationed at Fort St. John should make two patrols a month to Fort Nelson. This trip revealed how little was known about the country — or by bureaucrats. Instead of two trips a month it took nearly two months to make one trip. The officers landed back at Fort St. John on October 17, a total of 49 days — and they had been fortunate.

That far north snowstorms are usually encountered during the latter part of September or the beginning of October. On this occasion, however, snow held off until October 14.

The officers reported that the wilderness country was a trapper's paradise, with practically all species of fur-bearing animals. The portion travelled did not show any promise of minerals. The timber was chiefly spruce with balsam on the higher levels and cottonwood along the river flats. From an agricultural point of view it appeared suitable for mixed farming, although certain areas were apparently subject to late and early frosts.

Regarding the lost trappers, the Fontas Indians told the officers they could expect to find them dead. They had seen them the previous winter up the Fontas River without food. The Indians had given them supplies and pointed the way to Fort Nelson. That was the last seen of the trappers. (Their bones were found by Barber and Forfar three years later.) They had perished in the "great alone," not being sufficiently experienced to buck the northland.

Swift action followed completion of the exploratory trip. That same year a winter trail was cut through and an independent trading company established a post at Nig Creek. The following winter the Hudson's Bay Company opened a trading post at the Sikanni.

In Constable Barber's later years when he had risen to the rank of Inspector, he recalled: "For approximately 200 miles the Alaska Highway follows practically the same route which we took and therefore I consider that Constable Forfar and I blazed a portion of the celebrated highway before there was even a trading post between Fort St. John and Fort Nelson."

"On looking back, knowing what we went through, and the time it took to make the trip — namely 49 days — which can now be done by motor vehicle in about five hours or by plane in minutes, I am amazed by the change."

For Constable Barber, however, his association with Fort Nelson wasn't over. In 1926 he was assigned the task of trekking 300 miles in the bitter cold of Northern B.C. to establish a police post at Fort Nelson. Despite the hardships, his wife accompanied him. That story is told in Heritage House book, *Off Patrol: Memories of B.C. Provincial Policemen.*

Top right: Sergeant Sperry Cline.

Sergeant Sperry Cline —
One Of A Kind

He was noted for his dry humor and forthright
approach to police work, whether trundling a drunk
to jail in a wheelbarrow, sparring with lawyers in
court, or investigating a local resident who had
hanged himself, or "swung his last swing."

by Deputy Commissioner Cecil Clark

Of the cast of millions who have appeared on the B.C. stage of life
during the past century, time and public opinion have nominated

Hazelton about 1912. The police station is the building above.

only a few for an historic Hall of Fame. They are the unconventional, the courageous, the characters — the misfits, some will say. They are men like John A "Cariboo" Cameron who took $350,000 in gold from his claim near Barkerville but who was buried a pauper overlooking the once-rich creek; there was "Sea Wolf" McLean who became the central character in one of Jack London's best-selling books; there was Simon Gun-an-Noot, a Kispiox Indian who outwitted the B.C. police force for 13 years; and there was "Gassy" Jack Deighton who built a saloon on the shore of Burrard Inlet and founded Gastown, today better known as Vancouver. You can add a frontier packer like Cataline, cowboy-author Rich Hobson, priests such as Father Pat, and a sprinkling of stagecoach drivers, loggers, and miners. Politics, wealth and position play no part in this selection, and even though individual preference substitutes a name here and there, they remain a handful of highly adventurous characters.

To their number I add Sperry Cline, alias Sergeant Sperry Cline of the B.C. Provincial Police and "Dutch" Cline to his host of friends. He joined the Force in Hazelton in 1914 and when he retired 32 years later was one of the best known men on the Force, still remembered by scores of policemen as a disciplinarian, humorist and sage counsellor. Before being transferred to Victoria and the Police Training School, he spent many years in communities such as Hazelton and Smithers, a superb frontier policeman. He had a simple approach to police problems, some of his solutions quite foreign to the modern-day policeman.

As a senior officer in the B.C. Police Force I knew Dutch very well. Not, however, until I visited him in a Burnaby hospital in the spring of 1964 did I know — and appreciate — the practical nature of some of his solutions to these problems.

For instance when Cline was a policeman in Hazelton during World War One a saloon keeper wrote to the Attorney-General complaining that a merchant across the street was bootlegging. He pointed out that this action was not only illegal but unfair since he was paying for a liquor license and the bootlegger wasn't. The Attorney-General sent the letter to the Superintendent of Provincial Police, who passed it on to district Chief Constable Walter Owen at Prince Rupert. He, in turn, pushed it along to Cline for action.

Sperry called on the alleged bootlegger and showed him the letter, with the remark, "This is what the fellow across the street thinks of you."

Then he moved down the street and slipped into the first convenient alleyway to await developments. Finally, he saw the alleged bootlegger standing in the roadway, and — by the stridency of his tone — summoning the publican to an accounting.

"Well, sir," said Dutch in his inimitable style, "in a few minutes I was witnessing the goddamndest fight you ever saw in your life. Quite ... har-umph ... enlivened my afternoon."

"And what was the outcome?" I asked, thinking of the normal aftermath of an arrest for disturbing the peace.

"Well," said Dutch, "after their display of pugilism one could only report that it was a misunderstanding that had been amicably settled.

"You see, Nobby," he went on, "police work is fundamentally a matter of bringing people together."

That same afternoon I learned that using this philosophy, Cline engineered the surrender of Gun-an-Noot, the Kispiox Indian who is a legend in northern B.C. The saga began in 1906 with the discovery of the bodies of two white men, Alec McIntosh and Max LeClair, on a lonely trail near Hazelton. Although there was virtually no evidence, a coroner's jury decided that Simon Gun-an-Noot and his brother-in-law, Peter Hi-ma-dan, were the culprits since they could not be found after the killings. A search was started for the two, a search that was to last 13 years and cover thousands of square miles of wilderness north, northwest and northeast of Hazelton. Despite a $1,000 reward and the expenditure of over $100,000 (a vast sum when a Special Constable's wages were $75 a month), the men were never caught.

Cline decided to close the case. He succeeded by doing one thing — nothing. Even the wanted poster vanished from his Hazelton office. Then in 1917 Cline's old friend — fur trader and packer George Beirnes — met Gun-an-Noot while prospecting near the headwaters of the Skeena River. As a result, he contacted Stuart Henderson, a famous defence lawyer who had crossed words with Cline in many a courtroom battle. He spoke to Sperry about the possibility of Gun-an-Noot surrendering.

Cline said he would see what he could do. Through the bush grapevine he fixed a date when Gun-an-Noot would walk in to Hazelton and give himself up. But suddenly Henderson thought of a legal snag. If Cline was a Crown witness he would be subject to cross examination. In this event the probing would reveal that he had prior knowledge of a deal. So, when Gun-an-Noot arrived, Cline had to be out of the way.

By a strange coincidence, at that moment a train pulled in from Prince Rupert depositing Constable John Kelly. He handed Cline a subpoena calling for his immediate presence at the Prince Rupert Assizes. Kelly was to take his place during his absence. The next westbound train took Cline off the scene, and the following morn-

The Hazelton Police Station with, left to right, Stuart Henderson, Gun-an-Noot, and George Beirnes after the long-sought Indian surrendered.

ing Kelly, in the police office, heard an Indian at the counter say, "I'm Simon Gun-an-Noot. I've come to give myself up."

Kelly was just remarking "Give yourself up for what?" when Stuart Henderson walked in. "I believe there is a warrant in existence for this man on a charge of murder," he informed the astonished Kelly. "I'm here as his counsel."

There was a trial in Vancouver and on October 8, 1918, Gun-an-Noot walked out of the courtroom a free man. Several months later Peter Hi-ma-dan similarly came to court and was released.

I have already mentioned that Cline and Henderson had duelled in court battles. In that era in the rugged sink or swim policy of the B.C. Police, Constables prosecuted their own cases in court and without legal aid. In these lower court jousts, Dutch Cline more than once bested Henderson, who was also a character and one of the province's most capable defence lawyers.

An example of Sperry's composed and self-controlled courtroom manner was shown in a case remembered by Sub-Inspector J. A. Henry. He related the incident in an issue of *Off Patrol*, newsletter of the B.C. Provincial Police Veterans' Association.

On one occasion Sperry charged a man with consuming beer outside a dance hall. It was not exactly a brutal act and was, in fact, very common but nevertheless illegal. The man pleaded not guilty and Sperry ended up in the witness box being cross-examined by the defence lawyer. The lawyer admitted that his client had been in a public place and had been holding a bottle of beer to his lips. After this admission he asked Sperry: "How do you propose to convince the court that the accused was drinking from the bottle?"

Sperry considered for a moment or two. Then he adjusted the cud of Copenhagen snuff which he was hardly ever without and replied in his typical crusty drawl: "Well, now, if your client was gargling his throat with the contents of that bottle, he certainly wasn't spitting any of it out."

A conviction resulted.

In addition to Sperry's unflappable nature, his sense of humor was legendary. Assistant Commissioner of the B.C. Police, Bill Dunwoody, once told me about the first time he met him. It was in Hazelton about 1915. Cline was trundling a drunk to the lockup in a wheelbarrow. "The Hazelton patrol wagon," he remarked, with a grin.

Another local, Jack May, was familiar with Cline's "patrol wagon." Usually the main sound in Hazelton was barking dogs or braying mules from the pack trains. Occasionally, however, was added wolf-like howls accompanied by the sound of falling bodies or breaking glass. Dutch knew that May was on the alcoholic warpath and it was his cue for another test of strength putting Jack in the lockup. He always got him there — but it was tiresome.

Then one Sunday afternoon an Indian burst breathlessly into the Hazelton police station. "Come quick, Mr. Cline," he gasped. "Jack May — he hanged himself!"

"You don't say," said Dutch, spacing his words carefully, slight unbelief in his tone. "Where did this happen?"

"In his cabin. On the Silver Standard road — better come quick and cut him down before he die!"

"Now, just a minute," said the calm and methodical Cline, reaching for his complaint book. Carefully he ruffled through the pages until he came to the last entry, picked up a pen, dipped it in the ink well and enquired: "What did you say his name was?"

"You know his name!" exploded the dumbfounded Indian. "Jack May! Jack May! You know Jack May!"

"Ah, yes," muttered Dutch. "Jack May."

In the book he wrote the name, an account of the event, and the address. Then he enquired about the messenger's name and added that.

Having conscientiously noted Mr. May's dilemma, he then picked up his Stetson and sauntered out to the police car. Maybe it was the condition of the road that engendered a touch of caution for he drove to May's cabin at a safe and sane 20 miles an hour.

Perhaps this all sounds a bit uncharitable, but not to those who knew Jack May. Chuck Sawle, editor of the local *Omineca Herald*, reported the occurrence as follows:

"SWUNG HIS LAST SWING FROM A ROPE SUNDAY"

"John May ended his stirring career in a lonely cabin in the bush.

"John May died last Sunday and is now in the happy hunting grounds. His last journey was taken voluntarily without much regret on the part of other Indians.

"Last Sunday May and his wife Lizzie indulged freely in home brew until Lizzie went to sleep. Then another Indian and his wife called. There was more beer and considerable friendly conversation until John's dignity was offended and his savage temper went skyward. He turned them out of doors. Lizzie returned to her abode Monday afternoon and found John in a standing position but with a rope securely fastened 'round his neck, the other end tied to the rafters. He was quite harmless.

"On Thursday a coroner's jury decided that John May had hanged himself by the neck in a cabin on the Standard road half a mile from the mill; also that he was dead. The latter conclusion was arrived at after viewing the remains."

The newspaper account displayed a reporting flavor definitely lacking in today's newspapers but one which paralleled Cline's ability to express much in a few words — at the same time suggesting that much more was left unsaid. There was the time, for instance, when he was asked by an Inspector about the fit of a new issue of uniform. "The britches, sir," Cline drawled, "are maybe a mite tight under the armpits."

On another occasion when the same type of question presented some difficulty in reply, his pause ended with the observation: "Well, you might say the tie's a good fit."

When he was transferred to Chemainus after many years in the north — and outdoor plumbing — he was shown around his new living quarters by the Sergeant. After walking appraisingly from room to room he ended up in the bathroom. There, meditatively, he flushed the toilet, then repeated the process. Turning to the Sergeant he said, with a slow grin, "'Bout as near to heaven as a policeman has a right to get!"

Among Sperry's assignments when he was transferred from the north was Corporal in charge of recruits at the Police Training School at Douglas House in Victoria. The newcomers soon discovered that under his gruff, hairy exterior was a considerate person whom they came to regard with affection. By contrast, their opinion of Quartermaster Sergeant Bob "Bobby" Sims who issued their gear was quite different.

Sims seemed to delight in giving recruits what is today called a "hard time." Particularly annoying to recruits was his habit of issuing clothing in the wrong size. As Corporal P. H. "Spike" Brown later recalled:

"...I could never understand Bobby's attitude to rookies when they drew their uniforms.

"On a raw late October day in 1931 I stood stripped to my undershorts with other members of the Douglas House squad who were in the same condition by Bobby's command. We shivered in the dark coldness of a drafty unheated room of the Drill Hall while he issued our gear, which was often in the wrong size, necessitating much swapping between us to obtain reasonable fittings. When such was not possible, we enlisted Corporal Sperry Cline's intervention to ensure we would be properly uniformed.

"Maybe keeping us almost nude and teeth-chattering for the best part of two hours was Bobby's idea of toughening up recruits. But in my thinking it was senseless, as was the issuing of wrong sizes which caused waste of time and inconvenience, just as was the issuing to me of pair of Strathcona boots two sizes too small. These were exchanged with Cline's help for a pair more appropriate...."

Constable J. F. "Jack" French was among those with a warm memory of Sperry. "I remember standing aghast in the Victoria District office," he wrote in the B.C. *Provincial Police Veteran's Association* newsletter, "while dear old Corporal Sperry Cline answered the telephone. He was very much a down-to-earth man, disliked frills, and was impatient with those he suspected of putting on airs. He had a retired Colonel with a hyphenated name on the other end of the line, a type he held in some contempt, and was obviously pretending he could not understand the caller's repeated attempts to convey the spelling of his cognomen. I could hear the voice of the man on the phone becoming louder and louder as he tried to get his name straight with Sperry, while that wily codger provoked him by asking again and again, Mr. Who?, in the process spitting a little snoose in which he habitually indulged. Finally, Sperry ... gave me a little wink as though to say 'So much for him'!"

Dutch's comments and observations were delivered in a halting sort of nasal undertone. If the content often had the flavor of Will Rogers, the delivery smacked of W. C. Fields. But Sperry was not of another land, he was as Canadian as lacrosse and maple syrup, born and schooled close to St. Thomas in Ontario's Elgin county.

He was probably big for his age when he left home to cross to England on a cattle boat and, in his early teens, joined the British South Africa Company. This firm was much like the early day Hudson's Bay Company, except that it had its own cavalry. For this reason, in the late spring of 1896, young Cline found himself riding with the Matabele Field Force, 850 strong, through the rocky defiles of the Matoppo Hills, heading to the defence of Bulawayo. That spring, 12,000 war-like Matabele natives (Zulu in origin) had declared war on the whites and butchered some 300 isolated farm families. The slouch-hatted, bandoleered cavalry came riding to the rescue. The Matabele used a long throwing spear, following it up with a charge behind big cowhide shields to get to close quarters with a short stabbing spear. There was some bitter hand-to-hand fighting but by October they were battled to a standstill. Sperry stayed in South Africa to campaign during the Boer War until he was invalided home with malaria. During his service he won the Distinguished Conduct Medal but was always a little self-conscious about mentioning it.

Sperry arrived in Hazelton in the winter of 1904-05. While wintering in the riverside community he was approached by postmaster and pioneer merchant R. S. Sargent to make an emergency mail run to Kitimat on the coast, over 100 wilderness miles away. Of this experience he later wrote:

"Shortly after New Year's my partner, Gus Rosenthal, and myself left Hazelton with a toboggan load of mail, hauled by a six-dog team. Dog teaming under the existing conditions was a two-man job — one man ahead on snowshoes with a heavy pole breaking trail and testing the ice (of the Skeena River), the other, of course, driving and handling the toboggan.

"This trip proved to be one of the hardest that I experienced in

Until completion of the Grand Trunk Pacific Railway in 1914, the only access to Hazelton in winter was by dog team, a journey of from 100 to 200 miles. Sperry's first job in Hazelton was an emergency mail run to Kitimat.

my years of travel in that country. Thawing set in and it was necessary to test nearly every yard of soft and breaking ice. Later when we left the river, at a point several miles below where the present town of Terrace is located, to cross the portage to Kitimat, a heavy snowfall made progress slow and hard.

"As there was no-one in that part of the country it was a matter of making camp and the early darkness made it necessary to make camp early. Camp fires had to be 'rafted,' that is, two or more trees were felled side by side and the fire built on the fallen trunks. This was the only way to keep the fire from thawing a well in the deep snow and so become useless for heat or cooking.

"Another reason for burning camp fires all night was wolves. Many nights while camping on this trail we heard howling in the vicinity and on one occasion they prowled so close to camp that we could see the glow of their eyes. The dogs on this occasion crouched so close to the fire for protection that next morning we found their coats badly scorched."

On one trip he had an experience at Lakelse Hot Springs which could have been fatal. In one area the trail went over one of the springs, and as Sperry later wrote: "The vegetation, owing to the warmth, had been heavy and the windfalls of past ages were crisscrossed and piled up which, together with the dense growth of underbrush, had caused the snow to be held to a height of 12 to 15 feet."

Although the trail was well broken and hard, Sperry and his dogs suddenly dropped 15 feet into a muddy pool several hundred feet square. "I found myself floundering in a warm oozy mud with six struggling dogs, a clump of devil's club and a heavy toboggan load of mail. Fortunately my partner, who had been behind, came up and assisted in the rescue. First the dogs were hauled up one by one, then the mail, sack by sack, then the toboggan and finally myself. I had only received a few bruises, a skin full of devil's club needles and a mud bath, otherwise I was in good shape."

Later, in his B.C. Police service, Sperry was to find his early trail-blazing an asset. Though in summer a call to the wilds meant horse or canoe, in winter he was back to "mushing the dogs." On one particularly tough trip he logged over 200 miles to reach a lonely cabin on the Yukon Telegraph Line and bring in the frozen body of an unfortunate telegraph operator. (Described in the next article.)

It was in the Skeena that Sperry acquired his nickname. In his daily speech he had a tendency to mingle Cape Dutch and Swahili with his new-found Chinook — and it all added up to "Dutch" Cline.

In addition to his trilingual speech habits, Sperry had another distinction — there was general agreement that he was the most hairy individual to strike the Skeena in several decades. "He was a very hairy man, chest covered with hair and usually wore whiskers and never bothering about combing his hair, which was usually quite long and unruly," wrote his good friend and Bulkley Valley historian Wiggs O'Neill many years later. Sperry shared this assessment since he once wrote: "I was blessed (or cursed) with a remarkably quick and heavy growth of hair and beard...."

But, as Wiggs noted, he was also a "resourceful fellow who could fit himself into any occasion." Wiggs met him in 1907 in Port Essington at the mouth of the Skeena River. At the time John W. Moore, Jr. was looking for a pilot of a sailing sloop, the *Narbethong*, which he had chartered to ply the Lower Skeena River. Since the skipper, H. K. Freeman, knew nothing about the river with its tricky currents and channels he decided to hire someone who did. As Wiggs later wrote: "He marched into the Essington Hotel where a few fellows were sitting around the lobby.

"He sang out, 'I'm looking for a Skeena River pilot; anyone here know anything about the Skeena River?' Dutch was sitting in a big armchair. He sprang out of that chair like a shot, as he was getting low in funds and needed a job badly.

"He said, 'I'm your man. I know every rock, sandbar and current in her.'

"Moore said, 'By gad fellow, you're hired. Just the man I'm looking for.' So Dutch became pilot of the *Narbethong* — even though all he knew of the rocks and bars of the Skeena was what he observed from the frozen surface. But as I say, he was a very resourceful fellow, could always fit himself to the occasion.

"We used to see the *Narbethong* passing up and down the river quite often, Dutch standing on the poop deck directing Captain Freeman on his right course. As he always came up river at high tide or on a rising tide and always left for down river at high tide he was immune to rocks and sandbars as they were always covered with water.

"One day, however, John W. Moore was not ready to leave camp at high tide and was delayed, so they had to make this trip down river when the tide was about half run out. The pilot was on the spot for the first time as he was forced to keep in the channel. Dutch really got the wind up, and was wishing he really knew more of those rocks and sandbars than he did. A happy thought came into his mind. If he lowered the big centerboard which went down about four feet, it would kind of act as a feeler for him.

"He sang out, 'Captain, lower the centerboard.' In a very short time, on a cross current, he was off course a bit and the centerboard hooked on to a big rock and the *Narbethong* went up on her beam ends. John W. Moore just grabbed the mast in time to keep from going overboard. Mrs. Moore, who was in the cabin, got spilled around a bit. If it had not been for the ship's great beam, the vessel would have capsized. The centerboard slipped over the rocks and the boat righted herself and all was well.

"When Captain Moore gathered himself up, he sung out, 'Pilot, I thought you said you knew every rock and sandbar in the Skeena River?'

"'I do,' said Dutch. 'That is the first one.'"

Sperry became involved in police work in the same casual manner that he had become a river pilot, although he was far more

Two of the bank robbers killed by citizens during Hazelton's wild-west shoot out.

qualified to be a policeman. I think it was after he had put in a stint as mine boss at either the Silver Standard or Rocher Deboule that Hazelton's Chief Constable, Ernie Gammon, required a posse to help run down a survivor of seven men who had attempted to rob the bank at New Hazelton. Unfortunately for them the same bank had been held up six months previously by another gang and a popular teller murdered. This time citizens grabbed their firearms and killed or captured six of the seven bandits. Cline was one of the posse and remained with the force for the next 32 years. (See Heritage House book, *Outlaws and Lawmen of Western Canada, Volume One.*)

As a policeman, Sperry had to change his appearance since he seemed to delight in looking as rough and tough as possible. In addition to wearing his shirt open to the navel, displaying his mass of magnificent wall-to-wall fur, he usually needed a shave and never bothered combing his long and unruly hair. Nor did he bother lacing his boots, which usually had a pant leg tucked in the top. The effect was that of a stocky, muscular scarecrow which had escaped from some farmer's field.

"After Dutch joined the B.C. Police and got married," Wiggs O'Neill noted, "he kind of turned over a new leaf. He had to wear a uniform, and I always thought he had a terrible time getting into the new mode of dressing. However, he made the grade and became a quite respectable looking police officer and did good work at both Hazelton and Smithers, where we knew him very well."

But if he changed his appearance, he maintained his sense of humor until the last. When I quietly entered his room in the Burnaby hospital that April day he was dozing, a vagrant ray from the late afternoon sun lighting a pink and clean-shaven face, topped by bushy white hair that plumed backwards. He looked for all the world like a medieval nobleman or cardinal lying in state. However, with a handclasp and a word of recognition came the old Cline turn of speech that destroyed the illusion. He was recovering from a very serious operation and I said, "You've had a tough time lately, Dutch."

"Yes," he said, bringing his blue eyes into unflinching focus on mine. "I think I'll stand pat."

A month later on May 8, 1964, Dutch Cline handed in his badge.

It was also in May, although in 1870, that Chartres Brew, the founder of the B.C. Police force, died at Richfield in the Cariboo. He is buried in the pioneer cemetery at Barkerville and on his headboard is this epitaph:

"A man of imperturbable temper and courage, endowed with a great and varied administrative capacity, a most ready wit, a most pure integrity and a most human heart."

If the words had been written specifically for Dutch Cline, they couldn't have been better selected.

Sperry spent many years in Hazelton, seen above "warming a cold snap" in 1912.

Sergeant Sperry Cline spent many of his 32 colorful police years in northern B.C. where he made many long dog-team patrols and gained a lasting respect for

Six Good Men And True

During the time that I was Provincial Police Constable at Hazelton I made many long patrols throughout Northern and Central B.C. Many such trips were enjoyable, some were otherwise. For example, an employee of the Yukon Telegraph Line committed suicide at the Seventh Cabin about 220 miles north of Hazelton and the Coroner ordered the body brought into town for an autopsy. The region

was total wilderness, the only access a trail that for hundreds of miles followed the single line of the Yukon Telegraph which provided a 1,900-mile link between Vancouver and Dawson City in the Yukon.

This incident happened late in March and as the Skeena River was breaking up I prepared for a hard trip. Dogs and toboggan would have to be used and I decided to follow the Yukon Telegraph Trail instead of the river. By so doing I could travel light and no camping outfit or provisions would be necessary as I could put up at the operators' cabins along the way. This would be harder going than the river but the Skeena took a big bend eastward above Kispiox while the telegraph line took a cross country course between Kispiox and the Second Cabin, shortening the distance by 20 miles.

I had no dog team at this time and tried to hire a team and driver but none was available. After scouring the native villages I finally secured the necessary number of dogs, fortunately one of which was a good leader. Now for a driver. The Indians were nearly all out on their trap lines so I started canvassing the whites. Eventually Pete Enoch, who was about 70 at the time, volunteered to accompany me. I found that I had as good a trail man as I could expect to find.

The travelling for the first few days was hard as the cross country trail was rough and hilly. The snow was soft and the dogs, being unaccustomed to working together, gave some trouble for awhile. As we got further north the travelling improved and at the Fourth Cabin we took to the river. Between the Fourth and Fifth Cabins the line left the Skeena and went up the Slangeaze which we followed downstream to the Nass River. The travelling on the Nass was good and we finished the journey without incident.

We stayed a day at Seventh Cabin while I investigated conditions surrounding the death.

We were getting reports daily on the state of the rivers and it was expected that the ice on the Skeena would go out at any time. We left the next morning accompanied by Ernest Loring, lineman at the Seventh Cabin, whom I had summoned to the inquest as a witness. The weather was warm but we did not fare too badly until reaching the Skeena. From there on we had to proceed with caution at every step. Three days later, Enoch, who was more weatherwise than I, suddenly stopped, wet his finger and held it above his head. After some seconds he announced: "It will freeze tonight and we can run in the morning."

We arrived at the Second Cabin late that evening. It had turned quite cold and the weather report said that a cold wave was coming from the north and there would be a heavy frost during the night. This was music to our ears as we had been anticipating all kinds of trouble on the cross country run to Kispiox. We decided to chance the river next morning, even if it was 20 miles longer.

The linemen were most cooperative and put us up comfortably for the night. The next morning we were awakened at the first sign of dawn, found breakfast ready and were advised to get going while the going was good.

We started down the river determined to make it as far as possible that day. Even the dogs felt better — I was pacing them and at times had difficulty in keeping them off my heels. The load was light, only the corpse, a few pieces of physical evidence and emergency rations for two days.

We travelled all day with only short stops at noon and supper, then on through the long spring twilight until it became too dark to see our way. Having no camping equipment we built a fire under a spruce tree and huddled around it until it was light enough to travel again.

The cold weather continued and we arrived at Hazelton while most of the population were at dinner. We had travelled 90 miles in a day and a half. I think it was one of the longest drives ever made on that portion of the river in that length of time.

Two years later I had another interesting trip from almost the same locality. Word was received at Hazelton that an employee of the Telegraph Line had gone insane and must be taken out. It was at the time of year when neither dogs or horses could be used and he would have to come out on his own power. The difficulty was he refused to walk out either alone or accompanied by fellow workers. He insisted he had an important piece of work to do and would not leave until it was finished.

His chief mania was writing and the yearly supply of writing material was getting low. I was advised to bring a supply for his use as this seemed to be the only means of satisfying him. I took two writing pads and several pencils, hoping that they might be of use in influencing him to accompany me.

Upon arriving at the cabin where he was staying I soon discovered that it was going to take a great deal of persuasion to get him to come with me. After several hours conversation in which I accomplished nothing, he asked me if I knew how he would have to proceed to obtain a patent. I saw a ray of hope and explained that the easiest and quickest way would be to go to Ottawa as quickly as possible. While he was musing over this idea I suggested that the longer he waited the more chance there was of some other inventor presenting the same invention for a patent. This seemed to convince him that speed was necessary and he was determined to start at once.

What was he patenting? He, of course, could not divulge anything until it was completed. But he assured me that it would be the greatest boon to humanity since the wheel was invented. It would also be of great educational value — students in the near future could shorten their courses at schools and universities several months by simply possessing a copy.

We left for Hazelton the next morning. Seven days later as we were nearing Hazelton I began to wonder how he would take to confinement while being held for medical examination. Many deranged persons object to such treatment. I explained to him the danger of having his work tampered with if he stayed at a hotel and suggested that he stay with me at the police lockup. He readily agreed and worked diligently to complete his invention while there.

At last we started on our journey to the mental hospital in Vancouver, some 700 miles away. On the train ride to Prince Rupert he kept a sharp lookout for box cars on sidings and the numbers of many of them were incorporated in his notes. I had provided a

Opposite page: The Yukon Telegraph Line was just wide enough for pack horses or a dog team.

Snow along much of the line was measured not in inches but feet — many feet — as shown by 2nd Cabin north of Hazelton. The telegraph operator kept his supply of moose meat for himself and his dogs in nature's natural deep freeze. Temperature dropped to -60°F and colder for days at a time.

good supply of paper for his use on the boat and he worked at high speed so as to complete his invention before arriving in Vancouver.

A few hours before arriving in port he packed his volumes of scripts and seemed elated when he declared that the invention was completed to his satisfaction. He seemed so relaxed and free from anxiety that I ventured to ask what the invention was. He went to the door of the stateroom. After making sure no one was listening, he leaned over and in a confidential whisper announced: "It's an index to the dictionary."

Another of my experiences with the men who manned the isolated cabins along the Yukon Telegraph Line occurred during my first winter in Hazelton and left a lasting respect for our jury system. A telegraph operator stationed at Kuldo, 60 miles north, was found dead on the trail.

I was sworn in as a Special Constable by the Coroner to bring the body to Hazelton where an inquest would be held. The death had occurred on Christmas Eve. I left Hazelton next day, accompanied by John MacIntosh, an experienced dog musher and trail man. Tommy Hughes, who was to replace the deceased operator temporarily, also went with us.

It being early winter, fresh snow had been falling for several days, making it necessary for us to break trail nearly all the way. Upon arrival I met Hunter Corner, the dead operator's partner, who had found the body on the trail and whom I summoned to the inquest as a witness.

The Coroner at Hazelton at that time was a young Englishman named Hicks-Beach, nephew of a prominent British statesman.

The pioneers of northern B.C. at that time were not noted as great respecters of personage and double barrelled names were not popular with them. As a consequence, the young Englishman soon became known as "Six Bits." He, being a public spirited citizen, took on the appointment of Coroner when it became apparent that such an official was needed on the Skeena. Being of the Victorian era he was a stickler for protocol. His simplest duties were performed in a manner that would have met with the approval of the most particular court officials of that time.

When I reported to him on my return he advised me that I was to continue to act as Special Constable until the inquest had been held. He then handed me a legal document in which I was enjoined to summon "six good men and true" to serve as jurymen.

Since I was quite new in the country I asked my friend, Mark Carr, who had been in Hazelton for some years, whom I should summons. He suggested six of the oldest Omineca miners who were wintering in town, as most of them could do with the small stipend that was being paid for such service. Also it would give the old men great satisfaction to know that they could still be of service to the country.

I did as he advised and on the day of the inquest they all appeared at the old log building that was being used as police office and lockup. It was quite apparent that they were taking their duty very seriously. Grey heads had been carefully combed, beards trimmed and each was attired in his Sunday best.

Ezra Evans, a soft spoken, mild mannered old gentleman was selected as foreman. They were instructed at some length about their duties. Witnesses were then examined. The gist of the evidence was that some enterprising individual, name not divulged, had taken a cargo of liquor up the Telegraph Line a short time before. Many of the employees on the line had made preparations for a Merry Christmas. The deceased had visited the Third Cabin, 30 miles north of Kuldo, and had been given a bottle of liquor to take home with him. He was a young man and unaccustomed to drinking. On the way home he had sampled the contents of the bottle, become incapable of travelling, fallen into the snow and perished of exposure.

The doctor who performed the autopsy had a rather difficult job as the body had to be thawed and the means at hand were rather primitive. However, he told of finding a considerable amount of alcohol in the deceased's stomach.

When the evidence was finished the Coroner again addressed the jury. He pointed out that the evidence was quite clear and that they should have no difficulty in arriving at the proper verdict. I then accompanied the jury to the nearby hotel where a room had been engaged so that they could consider their verdict in privacy.

The Coroner had expected that they would be gone for only a short time. But when their deliberations lasted for a considerable time, he sent a messenger to enquire if they needed more advice or other assistance.

At last there came a rap on the door and I was informed that they had reached a verdict. Upon their return the Coroner called the inquest to order and asked: "Mr. Foreman, has the jury arrived at a verdict?"

"Yes, your Honor."

"Mr. Foreman, what is your verdict?"

"Your Honor, we find that the deceased came to his death by natural causes."

This was many years before the atom had been split but if such a bomb had been dropped in our midst it hardly could have caused more consternation. The Coroner was overcome. For a short time he seemed speechless, then he started admonishing the jury for returning an unwarranted verdict. When the Coroner became exhausted the doctor, still thinking of the difficulties encountered while performing the autopsy, added a few words of censure. Then the Coroner as a final shot, asked the foreman: "What caused you to arrive at such a conclusion?"

The foreman, still unruffled, replied: "Your Honor, we considered that it is quite natural for a man to get drunk at Christmas time."

I pondered over this reply for several months. I was satisfied that those jurors had not returned such a verdict for any frivolous reason, nor was it an attempt at frontier humor, as some had suggested. Months later when I had become better acquainted with the old men I was one day in the company of the foreman and two others who had been members of the jury. I asked the reason for their verdict.

They told me that the deceased had an elderly mother in Eastern Canada and they were not going to have her told that her son had died from drinking and break her heart. They brought in a verdict whereby the old mother could spend the rest of her days thinking of her son as a hero who had died doing his duty.

Since then I have often thought of that jury. I am still convinced that they were "Six good men and true."

Peace River Posting

When the author was transferred from Victoria to the Peace River Country, he travelled over two weeks by train, wagon, sternwheel steamer and horseback just to get there.

---

by Staff-Sergeant G. J. Duncan

In the spring of 1914 I was sent to B.C.'s Peace River Block to open the first Detachment at Pouce Coupe. A number of settlers had recently taken up homesteads on what was called Pouce Coupe's Prairie, after an Indian of that name. A post office had been established at the store of Hector Tremblay, a French-Canadian who had been trapping and trading with the Indians since 1898. Until recently he had been the only white man in that locality. About 300 homesteads had been taken up on the Pouce Coupe Prairie and the government considered it necessary that a police station be established in this new settlement.

On receiving instructions from Superintendent Colin Campbell at Victoria, I made enquiries regarding the Peace River Country, but could get little information. In fact, my superiors were doubtful about how I should get there The only definite information obtainable was that my best route was by way of Edmonton, Alberta, where the Hudson's Bay Company could give the best advice as to how to proceed. I was given an advance of money, a small supply of stationery, and, taking only a handgrip and pack- sack, I set out by CPR for Edmonton.

Here I found I could get to the Peace River by either the Edson Trail or via the Athabaska River and Lesser Slave Lake. The Edson Trail being bad at this time of year, I chose the Athabasca River route. Taking the train to Athabasca Landing, I caught a steamboat for Mirror Landing, then drove by wagon to Little Slave River. Here I waited three days for another steamboat which took me down the river and across Lesser Slave Lake to the Hudson's Bay post at Grouard.

From there travel was by wagon 85 miles to Peace River Crossing, on a bad road through bush country. I arrived at the Crossing in three days, then caught the *Diamond P.*, a riverboat, to Fort St. John, 160 miles upriver. This was another three-day trip because the river was in flood and it was slow going upstream. Our boat tied up when darkness came as there was danger from driftwood and sandbars. Swarms of mosquitoes invaded the boat each time it stopped, and we fought them off with smudges of smouldering leaves in tobacco cans.

The author, above and left, at Pouce Coupe Police Station in 1914. The lumber was hauled 100 miles by horses from the nearest sawmill in Alberta. He remained in the Force for 35 years, retiring as Inspector.

Below: With trappers on Rocky Mountain Lake. Their "canoe" was hewn from a cottonwood tree.

From Dunvegan to Fort St. John not a sign of human habitation could be seen along the river, and we seemed to be heading into a No Man's Land. On the second morning out the captain of our boat took pot shots at a bear swimming in the river. Just as it was climbing up the bank it collapsed. A row boat was put out and the bear brought on board. On the following day we had bear steaks for dinner.

Meat from a young bear is quite good, and during my sojourn in the Peace River Country I often found it a welcome change from bacon and canned meat. Between Peace River Crossing and Fort St. John the river varies in width from a quarter to half a mile.

In those days Fort St. John was just the Hudson's Bay and Revillon Frères trading posts on the north bank of the river and a log building on the south side where the Mounted Police had previously had a detachment. At the time of my arrival it was occupied by a B.C. Provincial Police Constable who had three government horses, two of which he turned over to me. Owing to rivers being in flood, I could not make the trip to Pouce Coupe by trail so took the steamboat downstream to Cutbank Landing which was nothing but a bay in the river where the sternwheeler put off passengers and freight. There was not even a sign board, only a trail leading up the high bank of the river through dense bush, and I had to hunt to find it.

After passing a restless night by a campfire, fighting off mosquitoes, I started out with my two horses.

The first cabin sighted was nine miles south of the river, from then on there was prairie with scattered settlement for 20 miles to the south. The prairie was about 200 square miles of rolling land lying west of the Pouce Coupe River, a tributary of the Peace.

There being nothing approaching a village, nor any certainty where one would spring up, I decided to establish my police station as near as possible in the center of a settlement on Saskatoon Creek. A log cabin was built by one of the settlers who rented it to the government. This little building served as a police station until the fall of 1917, when the police office was moved to where the village of Pouce Coupe had grown up.

Sizing up the situation after a patrol in which I visited nearly every settler, it seemed rather a mystery what these people were living off. None had been there long enough to raise a crop and markets were too far distant if they had. I soon found out that there was hardly a family which did not have some member trapping as a sideline. In many cases trapping was the sole source of income. Some excellent catches of fur had been made during the previous winter right in the open country where the settlers were located.

In this open country the chief animals caught were foxes and coyotes, which were very plentiful, largely on account of the fact that the whole country was overrun by Arctic hares, or snowshoe rabbits. One of the settlers who ran a trap line within a few miles of his homestead made a winter's catch which netted him close to $3,000, over three year's salary for a Constable.

Black, silver and cross foxes, considered rarities, were quite plentiful. Several had been taken alive and were being kept in pens by their captors who made applications to me for fur farming permits. Owing to the difficulty and expense of shipping wire netting into the country these would-be fur farmers built their pens of logs and poles. Live foxes from the Peace River Country were in great demand in Edmonton where fur farming companies had started. Some of the Pouce Coupe men who had caught fox cubs alive took them to Edmonton and sold them at good figures. One man received $1,800 for a good black fox pup which he had dug out of a den in the bank of a creek running through his homestead. Several others were sold at prices ranging from $300 to $1,000.

Up to the time of my arrival no game licences had been issued in this part of the province, but I had no difficulty in collecting from trappers and hunters. They all got their money's worth and, on the whole, were intelligent people, willing to uphold the law. In the fall of 1915 I issued 48 licences to white trappers, all of whose lines I recorded. I also recorded lines of four Indian trappers who were allowed to trap without licences.

In those days the Game Act did not provide for the registration of trap lines. However, a section of the Act ruled that a trapper who had established a line had prior rights to it next season if he were on it at a given time. If he failed to resume his trap line he lost his rights to it. The Act also provided that no one could set out traps within half a mile on each side of a line held by a licenced trapper.

Disputes that arose as to trappers' rights were to be settled by the local Game Warden or Constable. There being no Game Warden this duty was mine. I decided that the best way to settle disputes was not to have any. When a trapper applied for his licence I had him describe the location of his line, which I marked out on a map and set down in a book. This system of mine was the forerunner of a present method of registering trap lines. I believe I was the first one to bring it into practice.

By adopting this method there were very few disputes to settle. In fact the only ones that arose were when Indians returned to lines that they had run some years previously and found they had been taken up by white trappers. The Indians of that country had been allowed to trap and hunt without any restrictions. They would camp in a location and kill off the game within a radius of about 20 miles, then move camp to another site and repeat the action. When they returned to a locality where licenced trappers were operating, I had to explain the law to them and request they move to some other hunting ground further afield. This policy was not always to their liking, but there was plenty of room and the majority did their hunting and trapping on the north side of the Peace River.

On one of these occasions I made a patrol west of the South Pine River to Rocky Mountain Lake. Here three trappers — Ernie Knutson, and Nels and Hans Neilson — had trap lines. An Indian named Alexis was encroaching on their lines on the grounds that he had trapped there several years previously. When the law was expounded to him he agreed to move further west, but was not easy to convince at first. The round trip took me over a week on horseback, camping in the open each night except while at the trappers' cabin.

These three trappers had a good log cabin for their headquarters. On their lines they had small shelters made of logs and boughs, as their lines were too long to make the return trip over them in a day. They led a rough, hardy life, but were used to it. Knutson lived to 75 but Hans Neilson was killed on his trap line by the accidental discharge of a rifle when it fell from his pack.

During the six years I was stationed in the Peace River District many changes took place. When I first went there the nearest railway was 400 miles from Pouce Coupe, mail arrived once a month on pack horses, and there was no telegraph communication. I have often thought what a wonderful thing a radio would have been in those days. By 1916 a railway was completed to Grande Prairie, Alberta, 90 miles southeast of us and a telegraph line connected us with the outside world. The Canadian Bank of Commerce had opened a branch near Pouce Coupe post office, where there was a store, rooming house, livery barn, blacksmith shop and some other shacks which gave it the appearance of a small village.

(Publisher's Note: Pouce Coupe never became more than a small village. Extension of the railway in 1931 from Grande Prairie to a new B.C. community called Dawson Creek bypassed the pioneer settlement. Dawson Creek, however, was destined to flourish, as was a new community called Fort St. John some fifty miles north across the Peace River. Both communities had no direct access to the rest of B.C. until the early 1950s when the Hart Highway was completed.

(Today, however, the Peace River Country with its wealth of natural gas, oil, coal, hydro and agricultural produce is linked to southern B.C. by highway, railway and scheduled airline service. Population of the prosperous region is some 50,000.)

Sergeant Daniel Tweedhope and his dog, Salty.
The dog mourned so much after the death of the
Sergeant that it had to be destroyed.

Death Ends Colorful Career

Fourteen B.C. Provincial Policemen were killed on duty and several others had their lives shortened by injuries, among them Sergeant Dan Tweedhope. This obituary appeared in *The Shoulder Strap*, the Force's official journal.

The many friends of Sergeant D. O. "Dan" Tweedhope, of Courtenay District, learned with regret of his death. Sergeant Tweedhope had been in charge of Courtenay District and during his police career made a host of friends. Born in Scotland, he came to Western Canada in 1906. He served overseas with the Canadian Expeditionary Force during World War One and joined the Nanaimo City Police in 1921. He was taken on the strength of the B.C. Police when the municipal force was absorbed into the Provincial body in 1926.

He was known far and wide on the B.C. coast for his kindly disposition, his tenderness to young and old, and his firmness in dealing with law breakers. In addition, tales of Tweedhope's courage and extraordinary physical prowess will no doubt become a legend among British Columbia's police officers.

Over six feet tall and weighing in his prime nearly 250 pounds, Tweedhope and fearlessness were synonymous. He excelled in simple deeds among simple folk — the scattered settlers of the coast region, the hardy fisherman and logger whose standard of manhood was embodied in bluff Dan Tweedhope who had once been a logger himself. When the Knights of the Axe straggled in from the camps to kick up their heels, it was usually the giant figure of Sergeant Tweedhope who loomed in their path and cautioned them to "take it easy."

Of the scores of tales told of his physical might, there is no better example than the incident which occurred at Burgoyne Bay on Saltspring Island in the summer of 1928. A lady and her children accustomed to meeting the daily steamer in a small car proceeded down the wharf on boat day. In sight was the *Island Princess*, the small CPR steamer which called around the Islands. Suddenly there was a scream. The lady driver had mistaken her gears, and the car was headed down the ramp towards the edge of the wharf. Over the stringer went the wheels, but in the same instant a big

The fire which shortened Sergeant Tweedhope's life.

khaki-clad figure had leaped across the wharf. With his enormous strength he held the car from disaster until the astonished skipper of the steamer nosed his vessel into the dock. With the bow pressing against the car, he took up the strain. But for Tweedhope's instantaneous action, the car would have plunged into 25 feet of water.

On another occasion in late October 1934, Tweedhope, in charge of the patrol boat *P.M.L. 6*, was groping his way in thick weather into the entrance of Port San Juan. A sea was running, but he hoped to skirt the sand bar at the mouth of Gordon River and make a safe haven. With lookouts posted ahead, he suddenly felt the vessel touch. Reversing the engine, he tried for a deeper channel — but a following sea bore him off. Aground again, the seas slewed the vessel on to the bar and listed her heavily. Calm and decisive, Tweedhope gave his instructions for using a kedge anchor to haul off. But a sea swept him overboard.

He didn't know until the next day that he had carried away the railing and broken three ribs. Another man might well have been drowned. But Tweedhope managed to get aboard again and worked with the strength of three men in the pounding surf to make fast a big hawser to the nearby cliffs.

In July 1938, the Campbell River area was the scene of one of the most devastating forest fires in the history of the Province. Thousands of acres of timber was swept away in the holocaust, and settlers blocked the valley roads as they fled with their hurriedly collected belongings from the advancing flames. The police worked hard in this emergency, and none harder than Sergeant Tweedhope. Hung with a pall of choking smoke, lit here and there with the glare of unquenchable flames, the country for miles around was an inferno.

In the van of every dangerous situation was Sergeant Tweedhope — exhorting and leading crews of weary fire fighters. The weak he helped, the shirkers felt the weight of his arm. On one occasion a flagging crew could keep up no longer. A gasoline pump was required further up the hillside — but the weary men could struggle on no more. Tweedhope lifted the pump single-handed and staggered up the trail with it. Little did he realize that it was the final display of his magnificent physique. His lungs badly "smoked" and his heart weakened, he went on sick leave. But strain of the weeks of firefighting cut short his life. In 1940, two years after his forced retirement, Sergeant Tweedhope died. He was 50.

The Detachment Office.

Constable J. W. Todd.

Telegraph Creek — Frontier Police Post

From 1942-44 the author was in charge of one of the Province's most remote posts. There was no road access, and in winter one-man dog-team patrols of 300 miles and more was a routine part of a policeman's duties.

by J. W. Todd

At the head of navigation on the Stikine River in northwestern B.C. is Telegraph Creek Detachment. To reach it travellers disembark

Constable Todd's wife with the police dog team at Dease Lake during a 250-mile patrol from Telegraph Creek. Colonel is the leader, then Major, Buster and Martin. (See also page 138.)

Dogs packed for a summer patrol at Sheslay, 44 miles north of Telegraph Creek.

Sheep Mountain, south of Telegraph Creek, was a favorite haunt of mountain sheep, goat and moose. Poaching was common, the only stigma getting caught.

from a CPR steamer at Wrangell, Alaska, then travel 165 miles up the Stikine River. The riverboat journey takes anywhere from 2-11 days, depending on conditions.

The mountainous scenery includes plenty of game, chiefly moose, goat and both black and grizzly bears. The trip in the early fall, with just a hint of frost in the air, the foliage a mass of color, is one of the most interesting and delightful in the northland. Points of interest include the Great Glacier, The Canyon — often impassable in spring — Grand Rapids, Glenora and a variety of scenic wonders.

Glenora, just 12 miles below Telegraph Creek, was a scene of great activity early in the century. It was from here in 1898 that gold seekers started out over the Teslin Trail, eager to delve into the Yukon's treasure chest. Nothing remains now but one building, our police lockup. Its occupant during the winter months is an ever optimistic prospector, Bill Grady.

Glenora would no doubt have remained the main center of population had it not been for the construction of the famous Yukon Telegraph Line built during the Klondike rush. Its single wire line provided a connection from Vancouver some 1,900 miles northwest to Dawson City in the Yukon. It crossed the Stikine 12 miles further up at a small stream called Telegraph Creek. Anybody who wanted to send a message from Glenora had to travel to Telegraph Creek, and when the Yukon gold rush subsided Glenora's population moved to the "Creek." The material for the Government Agent's office and the Stikine Hotel were sent to Glenora, but later moved to Telegraph Creek and erected there in 1904.

As can be imagined, distance means nothing in the north. The Detachment, for instance, extends from the B.C.-Alaska boundary on the Stikine to about McDames Creek on the Dease River some 275 miles to the north, and south about 200 miles. There are only 76 miles of "road" in the whole region.

There is not much opportunity to get around in the summer for travel presents many problems. During the months of river navigation, May to October, river boats are the method of supply. From October to the middle of November and from April to the middle of May we are held close to the Detachment owing to freeze-up and break-up. During these periods travel conditions are very poor. Best time for patrolling is between December and the latter part of March.

There is a good deal of game work with approximately 100 trap lines operating. Depending on the amount of work (and the weather) dog-team patrols extend from a few days to two or three weeks. The police team I had was above average, and capable in good weather of 50 or 60 miles a day. The average patrol was about 250 to 300 miles, taking from 10 to 14 days. These were one-man patrols, and with a light rayon tent, a stove and a few essentials I could make a pretty comfortable camp, even in -30°F and colder. While I preferred winter travel under good conditions to summer with its mosquitoes, there were days of blizzards when I wished I had never seen a dog or a pair of snowshoes.

The log-cabin style headquarters at Telegraph Creek was quite comfortable. Built in 1892, it had an interesting background. That year the community felt the need of a police lockup to properly house a Constable and the charges that might come under him. At the time Robert Hyland's house was used as a lockup and the cells which he had in it were evidently his own property.

The contract for the new building was a simple one-page, hand-written document drawn up by Government Agent James Porter and Robert Hyland. Date of the agreement was September 9, 1892, with completion to be one month later. The cost of the combination lockup-residence was $400. (This building served over 50 years before burning down in 1948. The replacement cost $35,000.)

There is a limited amount of garden space in the settlement

and anyone garden-minded can employ spare time to advantage. With the long hours of sunlight in the summer, vegetables grow at an astounding rate. There are no domestic cattle in the area so people live off the country or on canned goods. Principal fresh meat is moose, with an occasional change to goat, sheep or birds, depending on season.

The population is predominantly Indian or half-breed. The Reserves at Tahltan and Dease Lake have less population than at any time in the past, the majority electing to live on the Casca Reserve at Telegraph Creek. Nearly every family has a trap line but the lines operated by white trappers are usually more productive as the white man goes in for fur conservation.

So far as general police work is concerned, it's perhaps more varied in a district of this kind. Actual work performed, as measured in cities and towns, would make the average policeman remark, "What do you find to do with your time up there?"

It must be remembered, however, that the Police Officer in the north represents several government departments. Besides being a Game Warden, he's also a federal Customs Officer, and at times, unofficially, a doctor, undertaker, guide and father confessor. And there are a lot of times due to isolation and the special circumstances when the usual rules of procedure are of little use. Crime as it's known in the city is a rarity. Poaching is a type of theft which seems to be a general pastime, and the perpetrator feels more disgrace at being caught than in being punished.

No description of life at a northern police post would be complete without mentioning the policeman's wife. Orchids are hardly enough to honor the city-bred wife who transfers with her husband to the northland. Many of the small pleasures that are taken for granted in the city — seeing the latest movie, having supper at a restaurant, or dropping in somewhere for afternoon tea — all cease to exist for the northern policeman's wife. In addition, her husband may be away on a lonely solitary patrol for several weeks during the winter. During his absence, on the wife rests the responsibility of the police quarters — no small task in long periods of sub-zero weather.

For the moment this part of British Columbia is a somewhat forgotten country, but the airplane and the radio will, I am sure, spur mining interest, and it will no doubt come into its own. The myth that the north is a tough rugged place in which to live is rapidly being exploded. There are some hardships, yes, but the people seem to be free from worry and live to a happier old age than the city dweller. I'll never regret my time in the north.

Because of the dedication of the Mayne Island Horticultural Society, the Mayne Island lockup is the only one in B.C. which has been preserved.

The Rowboat Policemen

In the 1890s transportation for officers on patrol in the Gulf Islands was very basic — shoe leather on land; oars and sail on water.

by Marie Elliott

Lying close to the Canadian-United States Border, the southern Gulf Islands of British Columbia include the larger islands of Saltspring, Galiano, Mayne, Saturna, North and South Pender and numerous small Islets. At the turn of the century, while boat engines were still being perfected, this marine district was one of the most physically challenging to police. Not only was law enforcement carried out on foot but often with the use of sheer muscle power — in a rowboat!

Overcoming many hardships, the early settlers had worked industriously to clear the land. At the end of 20 years they were justly proud of their island farms, well-stocked with sheep and cattle. But, unfortunately, sheep and cattle rustling had kept pace with the growth in ranching, and what was once a petty annoyance reached epidemic proportions. Home base for the thieves appeared to be the San Juan Islands in the U.S. The many protected bays such as Fiddler's Cove and Saturna Island provided ideal locations for the rustlers' clandestine operations.

After numerous appeals by the Islands' residents to F. S. Hussey, Superintendent of the Provincial Police, Special Constable Thomas M. Robb eventually was assigned to Gulf Islands patrol in March 1893. Mayne Island was selected as his headquarters because it had a wharf and post office and was centrally located on the steamer route between Victoria and the Mainland. Mayne Island House, a small hotel and store operated by Justice of the Peace W. M. Robson at Miners Bay, provided accommodation until a lockup was built in 1896. Robb was replaced by William McNeill in September 1893, and in May 1894, Arthur Drummond was appointed on a permanent basis, followed by Stephen Hoskins in 1898 and Angus Ego in 1900.

A police launch from Victoria assisted the men in patrolling the Islands during the summers of 1893 and 1894. For all other seasons of the year, however, and from 1895 onwards, the only method of transportation for the Constables was a 16-foot rowboat equipped with a sail. Efforts by Arthur Drummond to secure a steam-powered launch in 1897 were turned down. By 1911, however, all the Islands had wharves and adequate steamer service. Constables were allowed to use this public conveyance for their patrols, rather than a rowboat. Arthur Drummond's desire for a police launch, however, would not be fulfilled until the 1920s during the rum-running era.

Officially termed "Plumper Pass and the Islands," the district extended from the Canadian-U.S. Border to Porlier Pass at the north end of Galiano Island, and from the Strait of Georgia west to Vancouver Island. The more densely populated Saltspring Island was thus a responsibility, and from 1900 to 1905 parts of North Saanich were also included.

Travelling in the line of duty did not stop at these boundaries. Stephen Hoskins recalls having to walk from Cowichan Bay to Duncan in order to contact other District Constables, and all serious cases had to be tried in Victoria or New Westminster. When investigating a boat theft in October 1894, Drummond journeyed as far as Seattle, rowing to Waldron Island where he then caught the steamer.

There were few unusual deaths to investigate. Most were from drowning or natural causes, although timber clearing by the Japanese resulted in the accidental deaths of men on Pender, Galiano and Mayne. In handling what was the most sensational case of the period, the shooting death of recluse Barnard (also known as Marnard) Wenzel of Tumbo Island in 1903, Constable Ego displayed incredible zeal. When an item in the *Vancouver Daily Province* suggested that the wheels of justice turned slowly in the Gulf Islands, William T. Collinson, J.P., Mayne Island, came to Ego's defence:

"I made out the warrant and handed it to Constable Ego, and

although blowing strongly at the time, Ego left immediately in a sixteen-foot rowboat for Tumbo Island, twelve miles along the open Gulf, and in less that three hours had found Wenzel dead. By 10 o'clock that night Ego arrived here at the Pass with Captain Shultz, who he had picked up on the way. Two o'clock next morning found Ego on his way to Saltspring Island, ten miles distant, to notify the Coroner. Having fulfilled his mission he landed back at the Pass in the afternoon, at once setting to work to empanel a jury, and by next morning had everything ready, jury, grave-digger, and a coffin to boot — making the latter himself. All this forty-four miles was performed in a rowboat, right down steady rowing; and you say Ego travels by slow freight. All the same, if you have a swifter man on your staff let us hear of him and he shall be dubbed The Imperial Limited."

All three permanent Constables were outstanding men in many respects. The foregoing is only one of numerous examples of their dedication and hard work. They were shrewd judges of character, quickly learning to separate local feuds from legitimate complaints, and with a salary of only $60-$65 per month, were able to operate on a very slim budget. They accepted their responsibilities without complaint, and gained the respect of the Islands residents.

Constable Hoskins noted: "As a policeman, you looked upon any place you hung your hat as home. Everyone made you welcome. I always had blankets in the boat, and a certain amount of grub. Sometimes you'd strike a poor shack, pull in, take the best they had, and give 'em what you had of yours."

Seldom did the Constables take time off from work. To do so the Superintendent had to be notified and a temporary replacement found. It was not until three years of police work had been completed in the Gulf Islands that a lockup was deemed necessary. With steamer connections, a post office, and a central location, Miners Bay was the logical site even though locations on the other Islands had also been suggested. Arthur Drummond's friend and neighbor on Saturna, Warburton Pike, generously donated property situated 200 yards up the road from Miners Bay wharf, and Levan Cullinson, a local resident, was awarded the building contract for $320.

The 1896 Public Works Report published the following description: "Erected a lock-up 15 feet by 23 feet, with one room and two cells, cottage roof, walls of sized 2 by 4 scantling, spiked every 18 inches, and enclosed with rustic floors of sized 2 by 4 scantling, set edge up and spiked together and to sills."

The building plan was similar to many lockups built at that time, although cedar logs were occasionally substituted for building material elsewhere in the province. The single room in front of the cells was large enough for magistrate's court, if necessary.

By January 1897, the lockup was completed and within a month a Galiano resident, Henry Freer, arrested on a charge of larceny, had the dubious honor of being the first prisoner. Because the lumber had not yet dried out, Drummond borrowed blankets and a bed from Robson's Hotel so that Freer wouldn't have to sleep on the damp floor. Unfortunately, the prisoner spent a miserable week incarcerated before he was found not guilty at New Westminster.

During the months of January and February, 1897, Drummond continued to board at Robson's Hotel. Following receipt of hotel statements for room and board, however, Superintendent Hussey sent a reminder to the Constable that he should now consider the new lockup as his residence — no further charges for lodgings would be expected from Mayne. The Department supplied a stove and table and chairs, but it seems that a bed was the policeman's responsibility. Not until 1900 did Constable Ego dare suggest to the Superintendent that the Government purchase the bed of the previous Constable, Stephen Hoskins.

It is not known how many prisoners were confined in the lockup since monthly police reports for the period are unavailable. When headquarters for the Gulf Islands District was transferred to Saltspring in 1905 the Constables found the lockup near Vesuvius Bay in an awkward location for law enforcement since it was three miles inland from the Ganges steamer landing. Six years after the move to Saltspring, District Constable O'Hara wrote a long letter to Superintendent Hussey, requesting that Miners Bay, Mayne Island, once again be made the Islands' headquarters. He stressed the importance of its central location compared to Saltspring, that it had the only hotel in the outer Islands, and telephone connections. O'Hara was allowed to have the Mayne lockup refurbished and it continued in use for many years.

Eventually, the Mayne Island lockup and property were acquired by the Island's first resident doctor, Dr. Christopher West, who used the building for storage purposes. In 1970 his descendants generously agreed to turn over the property to the Mayne Island Agricultural Society for a Centennial museum project. There were over 70 lockups in use in 1900, but today this small jail is one of the few remaining in the Province. It is open to the public during the summer months and by special arrangement at other times of the year.

He stood 6 feet 6½ inches and weighed 275 brawny pounds — with courage to match. He was Constable G. C. "Jerry" Sharpe,

Tallest Man On The Force

by C. Birch

In 1924, two bandits held up a bank at Creston, B.C. A short time later, Constable G. C. "Jerry" Sharpe was advised that a man answering the description of one of the bandits was lurking in the railroad yards. After a short search Sharpe cornered the suspect, who promptly reached for his inside pocket. It was a futile move. Sharpe's heavy fist crashed against the man's jaw and he went to sleep peacefully.

A search of the recumbent form produced a fully loaded automatic pistol and $500 in American money. However, though filling the description, he was not one of the bandits. He nevertheless received a six-month sentence for packing a lethal weapon and a nicely knotted jaw for having the temerity to try to use it on B.C.'s biggest policeman.

In later years while on police duty in North Vancouver, Constable Sharpe received a frantic call from a citizen who stated that the man next door was threatening to shoot the first person who dared to cross him.

On arriving at the place, Constable Sharpe learned that the man had gone into his house. No lights were showing, indicating to the Constable that the man might be in ambush behind the door. He nevertheless took his flashlight and went in. Hearing a sound in the front room he switched his light in that direction and saw a man laying on a chesterfield, a pistol in his right hand. Sharpe leaped across the floor and seized the man's wrist, forcing him to drop the gun. After that the would-be killer was marched away.

Constable Sharpe's most deadly encounter with an armed man occurred in December 1926 when he was stationed at Elko in the East Kootenay. He received a phone call from the storekeeper at Waldo stating that the Chinese who operated the local laundry had not been seen or heard from for several days. As visiting relatives from nearby Fernie had been inquiring for the laundryman, would he please come and investigate. At this time, Constable Sharpe had his own car for police work and his wife often accompanied him on routine trips. After gathering all details, he left for Waldo, accompanied by his wife on what he expected to be a routine trip. Events were to prove otherwise.

At Waldo, with one of the laundryman's relatives, Constable Sharpe walked to a shack about 200 yards from the store. It stood near a river, and there was no sign of life.

Constable Sharpe and the man pounded on the door for a few minutes but there was no answer. Sharpe thought the door unusual. It didn't have the feel of a door merely locked; it was solid and immoveable, as if barricaded.

When further pounding and shouting brought still more silence, the Constable questioned the relative beside him on the possibility of the laundryman being away. He was assured not. The laundryman never went anywhere except to Fernie, and he hadn't been there for some time. The Constable next inspected the windows. He was surprised to see that they were all boarded up from the inside. He tried the door again and then threw his weight against it. The barrier didn't budge. The laundryman might be sick, or dead in his bed. He might be hurt and in need of medical assistance. In any case, the Constable considered he was justified in breaking the door down. One or two attempts convinced him that he would require some tools.

A short distance down the river a logger was working on a log boom. Sharpe went to the boom and discovered the man was an acquaintance named Frank McNab. Armed with McNab's crowbar and sledgehammer both commenced to batter down the door.

After a few blows, Sharpe yelled again. There was no reply. McNab started hammering with the sledge again, but Sharpe signalled him to stop. He thought he had heard footsteps inside. With his crowbar jammed in the door Sharpe listened intently, then called again. There was no reply. Feeling they had been mistaken, they again started to force the door.

The door bent and wood splintered. Suddenly three bullets ripped through the door and whistled past their heads. Realizing the situation had suddenly become dangerous, they withdrew.

Sharpe recalled the barricaded windows. He began to wonder if more than one man might be concealed within the shack, and for what purpose? He decided to leave McNab and the laundryman's relative to keep watch while he went and called his superior officer, Sergeant George H. Greenwood, at Fernie. Sharpe then returned to the shack.

While awaiting the arrival of Sergeant Greenwood with reinforcements, Sharpe wondered if a bandit had entered the laundry, killed the laundryman and was now trapped. He was still pondering when Sergeant Greenwood with Constables Donahue, Ted Davies and Game Warden Brown arrived.

The shack was immediately surrounded and warnings shouted for the occupant, or occupants, to surrender. With no reply, Sergeant Greenwood gave orders to force the door.

At the first onslaught a fusilade of shots tore through the door. Sergeant Greenwood immediately ordered his men to withdraw. He had a plan that might result in capturing the shack's defender without casualties. Going to the store, he returned a few minutes later with some bombs made of mustard, pepper and whatever chemicals he was able to obtain.

Sergeant Greenwood then climbed on the roof and thrust the bombs down the chimney, jamming in a sack to plug it. Just as he finished, bullets ripped the boards at his feet.

Meantime, Greenwood's men attacked the door with a pole. It began to splinter and opened a few inches. In addition to being reinforced with heavy planks nailed vertically, it was blocked by furniture and bags of grain. Finally the door broke into pieces and the men thrust aside the furniture and bags.

Suddenly a gun exploded almost in Sharpe's face. He ducked involuntarily and another shot rang out. The bullet hit McNab in his right eye. Then another bullet smacked into Sharpe's right cheek, shattering the roof of his mouth and knocking out 14 teeth. The bullet came out on the left side of his chin and into the crowd that had assembled outside. It penetrated the windbreaker of an onlooker, but did no further damage.

Another furious fusilade of shots came from the shack, driving the attackers back. Sergeant Greenwood, not wishing to expose any more of his men to further danger, decided to withdraw. Two onlookers supported the wounded Sharpe, while others assisted McNab.

After making arrangements for medical attention for his wounded men, Greenwood returned to the shack. There were no more shots and after a long lull Greenwood and the Game Warden went to the door. They entered and found only the laundryman, in a pit which he had dug to escape the gas fumes. He had shot himself in the stomach, but was still living. They brought him out and rubbed snow in his face to revive him but he died without recovering consciousness. Later the officers found over 90 empty .455 Webley revolver cartridges.

Meanwhile, Constable Sharpe and Frank McNab had been given first aid by Dr. Christie who had arrived after several hours' battle with snowdrifts and bad roads. An ambulance had been called from Cranbrook, 40 miles away, and they started their trip to the hospital. For the wounded men it was a terrible ordeal.

Sharpe and McNab had been hit at approximately 8:30 p.m. It as 12:45 before they were placed in the ambulance for their trip to the hospital. But their troubles were not yet over. A few miles out of Cranbrook, the ambulance ran out of gas. It was four o'clock in the morning before the stricken pair arrived at the hospital, nearly 20 hours after being shot. Mrs. Sharpe accompanied the men, who were alternately conscious and unconscious as the hours dragged by. The worst part of the trip, according to Constable Sharpe, was while the ambulance lay stalled in a drift while the driver walked six miles into Cranbrook for gasoline.

Dr. Green of Cranbrook discovered on the operating table that Sharpe's jaw, mouth and gums had been reduced to pulp by the soft-nose bullet fired from the .455 Webley revolver. Despite the havoc wrought by the bullet, Constable Sharpe made a full recovery. The only evidence of his brush with death was a small scar on the lower side of his chin.

Frank McNab, the logger who volunteered to help, was not so fortunate. He was a heavy, athletic man when he entered the hospital, but slowly wasted away. It was thought that his deep grief over losing his eye robbed him of the will to live. Whatever the case, Frank McNab died three months later. Though he gave his life in the cause of law and order, there is no memorial to him.

Constables Colonel and Martin of the
Telegraph Creek Detachment. The dogs
were official members of the Force.

Don Ellis and Reo,
the remarkable tracker.

Constable Jack Purdy's wife,
Margaret, and Rex, a half-wolf
member of the Police dog team at
McDames Creek in northwestern
B.C. Like Mrs. Todd at Telegraph
Creek, Margaret often
accompanied her husband on
wilderness dog-team patrols that
lasted two to three weeks.

Canine Policemen

Dogs were valuable members of the B.C. Provincial Police, especially in northern B.C. where winter patrols of up to 500 miles were common.

A MEMBER OF THE FORCE HAS DIED
by J. M. Rutherford

A variety of different types made up the strength of the British Columbia Provincial Police. There were tall men and thin men, silent men and gabby men. There were those who liked the north, and those who hated it. But all had one thing in common — a high regard for their corps and their profession. When an officer died on duty the report was listened to by his comrades a thousand miles away with a sense of deep personal regret. Perhaps this deep sense of comradeship was enhanced because these British Columbia law enforcement officers were so widely separated.

In March 1946 a member of the Force died doing his duty. Few men, except those who deal with the bare record of such things, knew that their comrade had passed over the Great Divide. He was a four-legged Constable who ate the government's grub, and in his day had taken to the trail in pursuit of many a law-breaker.

His name was Colonel, a sleigh dog who was attached to the Telegraph Creek Detachment on the Stikine River. The following extracts from the diary of Constable H. Jamieson record his passing. Jamieson started out from Telegraph Creek on March 18th on a 236-mile, dog-team patrol to Gun Lake and back. He completed his investigation, and on the homeward journey he recorded in his diary:

"March 23rd, 1946. Saturday. 8:00 a.m. Leave Nahlin on return trip. Guide to follow me as he has slower dogs. Lunch Mosquito Creek. Arrive Sheslay 8:30 p.m. Weather soft, will have to travel at night on frost from here to Saloon. Fed dogs and gave them four hours' rest. Miles 57.

"March 24th, 1946. 1:00 a.m. Leave Sheslay. Arrive Saloon 6:00 a.m. Rested dogs for two hours. Continue over Telegraph Summit where dog Colonel became ill, vomited large quantities of moose hair. Loaded him on sleigh and continued to detachment, arriving 2:00 p.m. Trail very soft, snow going fast on lower levels. Colonel died at 4:00 p.m. So ends a faithful career. Miles 44."

Colonel, who was six, had been in the police three years. Just a rookie by human standards, but a quarter of his life, as dogs reckon it. He weighed about 110 pounds, and when he first became a policeman he had to mend his ways. Constable Wallie Todd was his first boss at Telegraph Creek, and sensing some characteristic of leadership in the big fellow, made him team leader. "Colonel," said Todd, "was quick to heed words of command, never vicious, and an exceptionally good worker."

Constable Jamieson's diary shows how valuable and strong sleigh dogs were. They travelled for 12 hours on Saturday, covering 57 miles. Then they rested four hours, and from 1 a.m. Sunday to 2 p.m. travelled another 44 miles, or 101 miles in 20 hours.

CONSTABLE MARTIN RETIRES

Another member of the Force at Telegraph Creek was Constable Martin, shaft dog on the police team during the late 1930s and early 1940s. For 10 years he pulled his weight through snow drifts, up frozen rivers, along precipitous mountain sides and through timber. Ice, sleet, deadening cold have all taken their toll of the brave heart under the shaggy coat. Serving as friend and companion to the Constable on his lonely patrol, hundreds of miles from civilization, for days on end, through hardships which would make the city dweller flinch, the sled dog is worth more than his weight in gold.

Though Martin was robust and still in the best of health, he may not be able to travel more than 20 miles a day. Twenty miles! Those who have been in the army may recall what it's like to march 20 miles over roads, most of it on flat ground. Tough, wasn't it? Imagine these dogs pulling a loaded sled through deep snow, whiskers encrusted with ice formed by their panting breath. At times sharp ice cut the tough pads of their feet, so that they had to be bound up in little moccasins. Thirty and more miles a day the dogs travelled in rugged country, and they continued until completely exhausted if their master ordered them.

Martin's last master was Constable G. Redhead at Telegraph Creek, the only police officer between Prince Rupert and over 400 wilderness miles north to Atlin near the Yukon border. The Constable knew that Martin had spent all of his 10 years since puppyhood in police service, but though still willing, had reached dog retirement age. The arduous patrols that could last up to three weeks in weather -30°F and colder were just too much for the aging dog. Constable Redhead requested to Victoria Headquarters that he be retired from the Force and allowed to go to a home waiting for him. The men of the Department of Transport Weather Station at Dease Lake, B.C. had asked Constable Redhead for Martin if he should ever be retired. They promised a good home among men who appreciate a good friend and faithful companion at a lonely post. Headquarters acceded to Constable Redhead's request, Martin became a mascot for a weather station after his 10 years as a Constable with the B.C. Police.

While Martin served the Force in the northern wilderness and was known to only a few people, Reo in southern B.C. was known to hundreds.

REO, THE REMARKABLE TRACKER
by Harry E. Taylor

Reo was a handsome Doberman pinscher, a four-legged policeman well known to the public in many parts of southern B.C. He was an intelligent dog with an incredible sense of smell. During his 11 years of service he and his master, Game Warden Don Ellis, saved many lives and helped solve a variety of crimes.

One of his most uncanny exploits was the finding of an empty cartridge case. Experts claimed it held the bullet which killed Frank Hargreaves, who was found dead on his cabin step. With his eyes covered, Reo was allowed to smell a similar live cartridge. Then for four hours he searched in the snow, and finally found the empty case in a pile of wood chips near the cabin door. It was an amazing demonstration of canine skill and pertinacity.

Another demonstration was in 1938 when a woman disappeared from Enderby, leaving a note stating that she intended to destroy herself with dynamite. Reo, then a very young sleuth, followed her trail for five hours after getting a sniff at one of her shoes. With unerring sagacity he led the searchers along densely covered mountain sides until torrential rains obliterated all scent. The woman was never found. She left a signed confession that she had set fire to the newly built house of a neighbor, and there is little doubt that she carried out her self destruction.

Among Reo's many successes was a manhunt in the bush below Barkerville in 1941 after a vicious criminal called Smaaslet escaped from jail. With only the scent from a blanket used by the fugitive to guide him. Reo trailed the criminal in heavy rain and through almost impassable brush until, shortly after dawn, the police closed in. Smaaslet, almost invisible in the thick growth, started shooting. He surrendered after a brisk exchange of shots in which Reo's master, Don, played a prominent part.

In such way did a Doberman pinscher rise to pre-eminence in the difficult art of tracking. Many a harassed policeman had just cause to feel grateful for acting upon a suggestion to "Send for Don Ellis and his dog."

When thieves stole two cars in the Vernon district, leaving both wrecked, it was Reo who followed their trail. It went through Coldstream Creek, up to the railway tracks and down the road to where they were given a lift by a passing car Then, from the wreck of the second stolen car, he traced the thieves into the Military Training Centre.

Reo played a stellar part, too, in the trek after the bandit who grabbed $5,000 from the Pioneer Branch of the Bank of Toronto in

1942. In fact, there very few major crime cases in which the eager black dog did not appear.

All dogs, of course, have remarkable powers of smell, judged by human standard, but something else is needed before a dog can begin to think of emulating Reo. That faculty of scent has to be developed to the highest degree. There also must be a high brand of courage, and unfailing tenacity of purpose. Equally vital is the will to keep searching that little while longer when the going is extra tough, the scent is bafflingly elusive, and the searchers are weary. Then it is that most dogs, after trying a few false scents and feeling hungry and footsore, bark to themselves, "Aw, what's the use. Let's call the whole thing off and get back to a warm kennel."

But not Reo. He was persistent — and analytical. On one occasion, for instance, Don Ellis and Charlie Shuttleworth, a famed cougar hunter, camped overnight in the woods and decided to fish during the remaining daylight. They found, to their disgust, that the reel was missing from the rod. But Don did not worry. He let Reo smell the rod, then told him to "Git."

In less than half an hour Reo was back with the reel. He had also figured things out en-route back. He apparently tried to pull the reel by its attached line, but soon found that a fishline's yen for tangling is never so acute as when there are plenty of deadfalls and bushes around. So Reo finally chewed the line off short and carried the reel back to camp in his mouth.

On another occasion he found a pair of badly needed spectacles which had been lost around a fishtrap by one of Don's helpers. Persistent human search proving fruitless, Reo was sent for. He located the glasses in two minutes, his disdainful look plainly saying, "What's the matter with these humans, anyway?"

Reo always slept on his own rug at the foot of Don's bed, and he never went to sleep before saying goodnight. This ceremony consisted of his nuzzling against the bed until he received a reassuring pat on the head. One night in early May 1945 he refused to retire, even after his customary pat. He returned again and again to the bedside, and would only stay contented as long as Don's hand was resting on his head.

About 1:30 a.m. Don was roused by the blankets being dragged from his bed. By the time he had fully awakened and switched on a flashlight, Reo's spirit had fled from his fine, brave body. Aware of his approaching end through some mysterious intuition, Reo's only thought was to say goodbye to his master, the sole recipient of his unstinted devotion.

General view of Penticton,
and the author — before his
unexpected mid-street
donnybrook.

The Time I Fought The Champ

The police station was nearby and the prisoner most cooperative, so what could go wrong? Plenty, as the author discovered.

by Corporal P. H. "Spike" Brown

Late one summer afternoon in 1933, as I was leaving the Penticton Detachment Office, Nicholl's Department Store phoned to report that a man had stolen a suit of clothes. The Sergeant instructed me to drop into the store to obtain particulars of the theft. To my surprise I found the entire staff in a semi-circle about a heavy-set man they had backed into a corner, keeping him there with the threat of "weapons" such as a chair inverted lion-tamer style and a metal rod from a display unit.

143

It was obvious that the man had been drinking. Perhaps by what developed he could have been affected by some other stimulant as well. I placed him under arrest and conducted him to the street, intending to walk him the approximately two city blocks to the police station. I did not handcuff him since he seemed so docile that I felt it unnecessary. I wished I had, however, when we reached the sidewalk of Main Street. He suddenly dropped to the pavement and yanked my ankles, overbalancing me and bringing me down as though I had been tackled in a football game. As soon as I fell my prisoner (?) sprang to his feet and did his best to escape. After a short chase, I used his tactics and brought him down with a tackle. Then the ruckus began.

I received a series of stunning blows to my face as he pounded me with his fists. He was so agile that I couldn't hold him and we were rolling on the street as we wrestled. When I got to my feet he knocked me down with powerful lefts and rights that made me reel and see stars. In addition, I found I had to try to avoid his feet because he used them as weapons to kick at my groin or other parts of my body. Although I was taking a pounding, he wasn't having things entirely his own way. I was delivering some hefty punches, too. A crowd had been quickly attracted by the fracas, and in an impromptu ring formed by the inquisitive townspeople my opponent and I slugged it out.

My tunic was ripped out of any semblance of a uniform — minus a sleeve, buttons, and epaulets. I lost my Stetson, one of my eyes was bunged shut and I was becoming groggy. That guy could punch! It seemed apparent that I wasn't going to be able to subdue my intended prisoner unless I used force greater than my fists. It would have been senseless to have drawn my revolver. The threat of it would have been lost on the fighting-drunk man, and quite likely the display of a firearm would have caused some nasty complications. We had been trained not to unholster a gun unless we intended to use it, and the predicament I was in certainly did not call for that measure.

I was reluctant to use my billy club — we carried sprung and weighted leather-bound ones in special pockets of our breeches. I knew the police would be criticized for brutality if it was employed in front of the excited spectators, even though its use was necessary. But there was no alternative. I reached for it. Then I remembered I had left it on a desk in the police office. Rather than continue the fisticuffs indefinitely, I decided to call on a couple of men I had recognized in the crowd for help. The only response was jeers.

During the 1930s there were elements in small communities embittered by the Depression who held the police in low regard as symbols of oppression. The two men I had asked for assistance were evidently of that ilk. The fight continued. I recall knocking my adversary over the hood of a motor-vehicle parked at the curb, and being hit by what felt like a pile-driver. My wristwatch flew off and I saw a hand in the crowd snatch it. That was the last time I saw it.

In the meantime someone must have phoned the Detachment Office for about the time we were practically out on our feet, the Sergeant arrived with the police car. He and I battled with our charge until we had him in the vehicle and while we were transporting him to the station. Getting him from the car to a cell was a continuing struggle since he fought like a madman. Foot by foot we fought with him through the office, overturning desks and causing havoc in general until we had him locked up.

When our prisoner had sobered up sufficiently to allow us to fingerprint him, we radioed the classifications to Victoria headquarters. Back came a lengthy record of convictions, many of them relating to violence. Of more interest to me was that across the top of the list was a line: EX-HEAVYWEIGHT BOXING CHAMPION, U.S. NAVY.

Although I have forgotten the man's name, I do remember that he was most ingratiating once sober, apologizing profusely for his behavior when I arrested him. His friendly, fawning overtures were a cover for his real character, however. As an example, although we could not prove he was responsible, we knew he stole a table knife from the equipment used to feed the jail's occupants, and on the concrete cell floor honed it to razor sharpness, as a stiletto. We learned from another prisoner that "The Champ," as we had come to call him, intended to use that knife in an escape attempt.

When he was taken before the magistrate for preliminary hearing he pleaded to be spared the ignominy of handcuffs, but I made sure he wore them and threatened to add leg-irons if he stepped out of line. The night of the fight both the Sergeant and I had to change into fresh uniforms, and the next morning both of us, as well as the prisoner, displayed battle marks. The prisoner and I had sundry lumps and gashes about our heads and each sported a gorgeous black eye. At the subsequent trial the ex-champ received several years for resisting arrest and theft. The two men who wouldn't help me were charged with refusing to assist a police officer on his request in the pursuit of his duty and drew heavy fines.

Throughout British Columbia scores of trappers and prospectors have died in the wilderness, their lonely deaths unrecorded. An exception was

The Diary of Despair

Article and photos by Ronald Dodds

It was April 3, 1940. At the community of Zeballos on the Central West Coast of Vancouver Island, Constable Nelson J. Winegarden was about to be confronted with the duty most disliked by B.C.

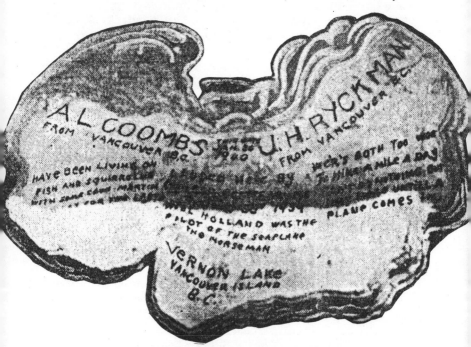

As the trappers' fight against starvation became more hopeless, on January 30 they burned a message into a fungus which they attached to the outside wall. It read, in part: "We're both too weak to hike a mile a day. Can't do nothing but stay here until a plane comes in...."

Opposite page: Interior of the cabin and the cabin itself. The trappers' makeshift wharf and canoe are at lower center. On the wall near the window is the fungus.

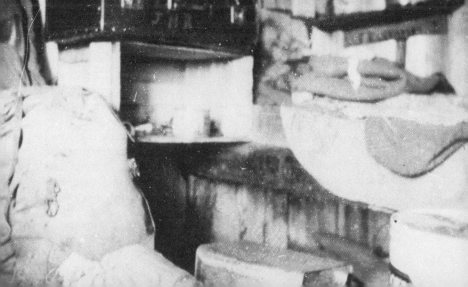

Provincial Policemen — removing the remains of people who have been dead for weeks or months.

The day previously pilot Jack Hames of Ginger Coote Airways had landed on Vernon Lake and taxied to a small log cabin owned by trappers James Ryckman and Lloyd Coombs. They had been flown in the previous July with 1,500 pounds of food. When they left Zaballos they had assured Postmaster George Nicholson, who was also the agent for Ginger Coote Airways, that they would hike out in the spring and that their food was more than sufficient to last.

But as Pilot Hames approached the rough jetty in front of the silent cabin he saw two pieces of white cloth fluttering in the breeze, a distress signal. He tied up his float plane and walked to the cabin, aware of an overwhelming silence. On the cabin door, laboriously burned into a large fungus, was a message:

"A. L. Coombs and J. H. Ryckman, from Vancouver, B.C. This date, January 30, 1940. Have been living on fish and squirrels with some coon, marten for the last... (unintelligible). We're both too weak to hike a mile a day. Can't do nothing but stay here until a plane comes in."

The cabin door was partly open and Hames pushed his way inside, aware that something had gone terribly wrong. Both trappers were dead in their bunks, little more than skeletons. (Their weight was later put at about 50 pounds each.)

At the time I was a young newspaperman in the Vancouver Bureau of British United Press, awaiting acceptance into the Royal Canadian Air Force. When news of the tragedy became known I was sent to Zeballos to cover the story. The next day Hames left to bring in the bodies and I was aboard with Constable Winegarden and Coroner Ralph Thistle.

As the cabin's door, hanging slightly ajar, was opened a cloud of small chattering birds fluttered out, apparently enticed by a vain hope of food within.

On the left were two bunks, one on each side of the cabin, and each held a grim sleeper. Next to the door lay Coombs, doubled up on the blankets, arms flung out and a rifle at his feet. Shot through the head, he had apparently sat on the edge of the bunk after his partner's death, placed the gun between his knees and pulled the trigger.

Opposite him lay Ryckman, swaddled in blankets, his head propped up on pillows. He seemed to stare in a fixed gaze at the door, as if expecting last-minute aid, a look of utter hopelessness and untold suffering on his shrunken features. His face was uncovered, Coombs apparently having been to weak to pull up the blankets that covered him.

Evidence of their determined struggle to keep alive was plentiful.

Two full five-gallon pails of water stood at the opposite end of the cabin where they did their cooking. Obtained, as we later learned from their diary, by crawling on hands and knees to the lake, it was never drunk.

Only food we found was a little tea in a jar on a shelf. Flour sacks were beaten to yield their last particle of flour and containers of sugar, rice, peanut butter and other foods had been cleaned of the last crumb. Nothing eatable had been overlooked except the tea, which they must have been too weak to brew.

Also used as a last extremity was the carcass of an eagle, mounted on the outside wall. The meat had been scraped from its wings.

Among their personal possessions was a diary, its daily entrees chronicling their desperate battle against starvation, and two letters. One, written by Ryckman about March 1, was to his family in Vancouver:

"Dear son and daughter, also my dear son.

"Well, Albert, this may be goodbye forever," it ran in part, "as we can't hold out for more than another week ... (Ryckman died March 17 according to Coomb's entry in the diary). Food all gone so we have been living on fish, squirrel, marten, eagle, coon, and everything we could get ... we caught canaries that flew in open door and cleaned them and ate them ... today we had seven that is all we had to eat ... I hope a plane lands here soon ... Lloyd getting weaker all the time ... we are slowly starving to death...."

The letter, written in ink on a tablet of notebook paper, was unsigned and apparently unfinished.

Coomb's message told a similar tale of despair and misery.

Dated Jan. 31, it was addressed to his mother and father:

"This is a last note just in case we don't get out of here alive," it ran. "Many a night I couldn't sleep thinking about home, but these nights I go to bed praying for a plane and for you to hear my voice ... you are entitled to half the fur ... so this is goodbye ... God bless you both as I've always loved you ... Your loving son, Lloyd."

The diary and my stories and photos of the tragedy appeared in *The Vancouver Sun* and many other newspapers throughout North America. The first entry appeared on November 25 with a notation that "We got three squirrels and six trout today. Jim's baking biscuits tonight. I took a bath. The weather is good, just foggy. That's better than rain."

On November 28 the weather changed and for several weeks storm after storm blew in from the Pacific, leading to what would be one of the wettest winters on record. Cold and snow later added to their misery. The entries for December 2, 3 and 8 indicated that the trappers were already in trouble:

Constable Winegarden, Coroner Ralph Thistle and, on the plane, reporter Ronald Dodds.

The community of Zeballos, below, was 25 miles from the trappers' cabin.

"Dec 2.—I set a trap over 1500 foot path to "N" (Nimpkish) River from "K" Lake. Came up river to V (Vernon) Lake. Rained all day. The trail was flooded out. I had to wade up to my waist a dozen places. I didn't think I would make it, but by the skin of my teeth I did. Jim got two martens and a coon down the lake today.

"Dec. 3.—We went over across the lake today. Got three martens. Rained heavy all day. If it ever stops raining it will be a miracle. We had the coon for supper yesterday and finished it for lunch today. That's the first meat we've had in here. My legs are still shaky from yesterday. Jim has another boil coming on his wrist.

"Dec. 8—Rained heavy all morning. Wind storm started about 9 a.m.; lasted about four hours. The lake was as rough as the ocean and waves washed the canoe clean off our 40-foot slope. Thunder and lightning in afternoon, with some hail. Cleared up a little after that (blue sky), but the rains pouring down again right now (9:30 p.m.). Got one marten right by the cabin door.... We're pretty near figuring our grub by the meals right now; that's how low it is."

The December 3 notation about eating coon (racoon) — an animal they wouldn't normally eat — and their statement that it's "...the first meat we've had in here..." is ominous. It indicates that in the previous five months they had had no success in shooting game. Is this the reason why their food supply was so low that "We're pretty near figuring our grub by the meals...." when they took in enough to last at least another five months? Does Coomb's reference to his shaky legs and Jim's boil indicate that perhaps they were already undernourished?

Also because of Coomb's shaky legs and the continuing storm pattern were they reluctant to try hiking out? They would be faced with rain-soaked underbrush, overflowing streams and flooded swamps and lowlands, all the time being soaked in downpour.

By December 15 there had been no improvement in the weather and their food gone:

"Dec. 15—Rained off and on all day with hail and wind. Jim got six trout in afternoon. We had a light breakfast and nothing more until four p.m. when we had fish. Cooked the last mess of beans today. Rice was finished last Sunday. We have one meal of porridge left, a few prunes and a couple of pounds of flour. To eat good we could finish it all in a couple of days. We're praying a plane will come in.

"Dec. 16—Rained all day. Tried fishing — no luck. I had two meals today and half-ration meals at that. We ate the last of the beans. If the weather doesn't clear so we can catch a lot of fish I guess we'll be eating nothing pretty darn soon."

The year end brought no change in the weather or promise of improvement in their starvation rations. They were now virtually totally dependent on fish they caught but they were generally so small that "about half a dozen were required to make anywhere near a meal for one person."

"Dec. 31—New Year's Eve, and it's seeing the old year out with rain. It rained like the devil all day. We both fished today and only got one small trout each. We had coon for supper up until today....

"Jan. 1, 1940—Jim went over to the line across the lake. Got one marten. We both fished and got four trout. We had coon for breakfast (coon meat two meals), had the last can of corn for lunch with two trout. Jim shot a mud hen yesterday and we had it for supper tonight. I surprised him with a five pound can of flour I had cached. That's all we have left for grub.

"Jan. 2—Jim went around the lake today. He got a weasel and two trout. I fished all day and never got a darn thing. We ate the trout tonight, so we have to get out in the morning and fish for our breakfast. It rained like the devil all day. The lake has been rising since yesterday."

By the end of the first week in January it must have been obvious to the marooned trappers that they couldn't hike out. On January 6 Coombs wrote that "I got pretty weak in the knees, rubbed them with electric oil tonight." Then next day he noted: "My legs are pretty shaky."

On January 8 they were cheered because the "...sun shone for about two hours. The last day it was clear was when we saw the plane Oct. 30." Next day, however, they faced a new obstacle — snow. By January 19 neither the weather nor their food supply had improved:

"Friday, Jan. 19—Got a mud hen and two trout. Jim fished all day; got none. Shot two squirrels. We had a squirrel breakfast; one-half a trout and one-half a marten each for lunch. One-half a trout, two squirrels each for supper. Had the rest of the marten before going to bed. Jim says of all the years he's trapped this is the first marten he'd had to eat. It tastes pretty darn good, too. Weather clear all day, sunshine.

"Saturday, Jan. 20—Jim went around the lake today. Fished all the way; got six big trout. Left at 8 a.m., back at 4 p.m. Had a big feed of fish then. I fished all day; got three trout. Shot two squirrels. Jim got one squirrel in a trap. Snowed all afternoon. This weather is darn cold out in the boats. Our hands get so cold sometimes we can hardly bait our hooks. We have to thaw out our hands when we get in before there is feeling enough in them to clean the fish.

"Monday, Jan. 22—I went over the line down the river; got skunked. Shot three squirrels. I got one trout, Jim got five. Jim got a big eagle in a trap. It stretched 82 inches from tip to tip. Jim was pretty sick in the stomach all day.

"Tuesday, Jan. 23—Jim got seven trout today and I got 10. That's the most I've got in a day yet, some of them pretty small. Rained most of the day.

"Wednesday, Jan. 24—Jim got four trout and I got three. Windy and cold all afternoon.... The eagle we got weighed seven pounds. I'm saving the wings and Jim the tail and claws. We're going to try eating it.

"Thursday, Jan. 25—We got three trout and one squirrel each today; the trout were all small. We had the eagle for lunch; it was filling. Snowed last night. Here's hoping we do better at fishing tomorrow.

"Friday, Jan. 26—Jim got three trout today and I got four. Rained most of the day and all last night. We had two meals today, one small trout, a squirrel each for breakfast at 9 o'clock; a trout and one-half each for supper at 5 o'clock.

"Jan. 27—Windy and raining hard all day. Too rough for the canoe. Jim tried fishing all afternoon, got none. We had two small trout each for breakfast, boiled. We skinned out the wings of the eagle I had nailed to the cabin and got what little meat we could from them. We got the neck we had thrown out and boiled that up. We ate that at 8 o'clock, saving the soup for breakfast. We're praying to God a plane comes in pretty darn soon.

"Jan. 28—Raining heavy all day and all last night. The fish wouldn't bite worth a darn. I got three small ones, Jim never got a nibble. We had a cup of soup off the eagle remains we boiled this morning. Had one trout between us at 11 a.m. The other two at 5:30 p.m. It cleared up just now; stars out 8 p.m.

"Monday, Jan. 29—We nearly had nothing to eat today until 6 p.m., one squirrel each that I got in the morning. We never got a fish today. We got some fish heads and tails on to boil. We're going to try it anyway; an empty stomach is willing to try anything. It was clear most of the day, sunshine and foggy in the morning. P.S.—We just ate some of the fish heads. It was pretty damn good too. Some of them were laying out for four or five days, so this will give you an idea of what hunger is. Jim is going to have to watch his boots or I'll be boiling them up. The fish guts were in the pot, too.

"Tuesday, Jan 30—We just had our first taste of food today at 8 p.m. We had five squirrels and a very small duck. The whole works would hardly make a good meal for one. We never got a fish today or even a nibble. We're saving the soup of the squirrels and duck for breakfast. Weather good, clear all afternoon, foggy in morning. The both of us have got so weak that its hard work to carry up a pail of water or an armful of wood."

February brought no change in the terrible weather. For February 3, 4, 5, 6, 8, and 9 the first entry in the diary was "Rained all day." On the 7th there had been an improvement since it had "Rained off and on all day." Fish continued to be their main food, although they had to work 10 or more hours a day to catch enough barely to survive:

"Feb. 10—Had 4 small fish heads stewed up each for breakfast; two small trout for lunch that Jim got in the morning. Both fished all day, that's what we got. One squirrel between us for supper. If there is a Lord God in Heaven he's forgot us poor fellows.

"Feb. 11—The both of us fished all around the lake and I got 10, Jim four. We cooked four on the way. Started without any breakfast. Cold and foggy all morning, clear in the afternoon, rained at 4 o'clock. Left here at 8:30 a.m. and back at 7 after dark, so there's a long, hard day for a couple of meals. Jim looked at traps on the way.

"Feb. 12—Windy all morning, white caps all over the lake. Rained all afternoon. Jim fished all afternoon, got two trout. I felt too damn weak and sick to go outside. Had one trout each for breakfast, fish heads for lunch and a trout each for supper. It would take just about half a dozen trout this size to make anywhere near a meal for one.

"Feb. 15—Weather good, foggy and cloudy, no rain. Both tried fishing, never got nothing. Am so weak in the legs I don't think I could walk 100 yards. I stayed in the cabin most of the day. Jim looked at four traps down the river. We had two trout each for breakfast, some heads and some soup off them for lunch. Three trout each for supper. The trout were so small there were about two good mouthfuls to each one. If we can make it we're both going around the lake tomorrow. It seems to be the only chance of getting any fish at all.

"Feb. 16—Rained heavy and windy all last night and today I'm so weak in the legs I didn't go outside. I laid on my bunk all day. We never had a damn thing to eat until three o'clock. Jim gathered up the coon guts that was laying outside and an old rotten helldiver duck that's been laying outside since before Christmas. We boiled them up in baking soda. It was pretty rank but we ate it anyway. We've been eating a few yeast cakes, they are old and hard to belly too, but they help a little. We have three left; I guess we'll eat them tonight. All we have is a little tea left but that's some help. Jim is going to try fishing up the lake tomorrow if he can make it. All I can do is stay here and pray that he gets a few fish and pray for a plane.

"Feb. 17—Well, here it is four o'clock and nothing to eat today. Jim went out this afternoon, tried fishing, no luck. The rain is still pouring down today and they won't bite in it at all. Jim is getting in a bunch of wood now while he's able to. He packed a bunch of clothes in tins this morning so we'll be that much ready if a plane does land here. I haven't been out of my bunk over two hours to-day. We tried cooking the coon skins but can't get the hair off, so I guess we're out of luck at that, too.

"Feb. 18—Rained all morning; stopped in afternoon. Clouds breaking a little now, 4 p.m. Jim's been out since one o'clock fishing. He got one small one this morning; we had that between us at noon. I caught three canaries this morning. It's a crime to do it, but we're going to boil them. They should make one-half cup of broth each. I've been out of my bunk only a few minutes at a time today. It's all I can do to stand on my legs at all, Jim got back at 5 p.m.; got nothing. We're just eating the canaries 6:30 p.m., so there's our food for today—three canaries and one small trout.

"Feb. 19—I shot a bluejay at the cabin door this morning, had that boiled at 10:30. Jim got two squirrels in the morning and one trout. Had them at one o'clock, used last scrap of grease. I've got nine canaries on boiling now at 4:30 p.m. Jim's out fishing, been out all day. I'm feeling a little better today, only legs I'd be out fishing, too. If it wasn't for Jim I'd be laying here starving to death. We're only getting a couple of mouthfuls a day but Jim says where there's life there's hope. Jim just got back at 5 o'clock, no fish; he's just about all in...."

By the third week of February both men knew that unless help arrived, their survival chances were slim. On February 21 Coombs observed: "They say have patience, don't swear and pray, but, by God in Heaven, it doesn't do us a damn bit of good." Contributing to their feeling of hopelessness was the weather:

"Feb. 23—Jim cooked the coon skin this morning, had it at noon, then he went out fishing, it snowed all last night and this morning. I got the coon skin on boiling now so after today we won't even have them to chew on. Jim just came in, we ate the coon skin, it was the smallest we had, no fish. Jim just got back 6 p.m. got one trout and picked some cranberries so thank the Lord for that, I don't know how he keeps going but he does.

"Sat., Feb. 24—2:30 p.m. and I just got out of my bunk feeling pretty dizzy, have to lay down again. Sometimes I don't care if I eat or not and other times its just a torturous pain. Jim caught two nice trout this morning and two canaries.... He came in at noon, cooked the fish and we ate (me in bed) then he went right out again.

"Feb. 26—Snowed all morning, rain and snow this afternoon. Tried fishing; no luck, so had tea for breakfast, tea for dinner and tea for supper....

"Feb. 27—Jim's legs swole up twice their size last night. Tried fishing again today, no luck. Got some more cranberries and 15 canaries. I haven't been out of bed for four days. Jim got a raven out of a trap this afternoon so we'll have another mouthful today.

"Feb. 28—It (Ryckman starts writing) rained all day. Lloyd is still in bed. I caught seven canaries this morning. That is all we had to eat today. My legs are badly swollen to my hips.

"Feb. 29—Last day of the month. Rained in spells all night. I caught 10 canaries with salt on doorstep. Cleaned and boiled them and we had them at 12:30 noon. Caught two more this afternoon and managed to get one trout. One quarter pound trout. So we had them separate. My legs are still badly swollen from feet to hips.

"March 1—Rained all day. Caught 15 canaries today, cleaned and ate 10 of them. Lloyd is no better. We are starving to death slowly. No fish today. My legs are still swollen badly."

By now the trappers' physical condition was deteriorating rapidly. Coombs was more and more confined to his bunk, while Ryckman's legs had swollen so badly that he could no longer get into the boat, ending the supply of small fish that was barely keeping them alive. Their main food was now the small canary-sized birds that they enticed into the cabin. Although the weather had improved, rain still fell nearly every day:

"March 3—Rained all day; not able to go out in boat to fish. Legs swollen to hips, badly. Hard time to get enough wood to burn. Caught five canaries today. That is all we had to eat today. Lloyd is no better.

"March 4—No rain today, little sunshine. Caught 67 canaries. Lloyd was up for two hours today, first time since over a week. My legs are getting worse all the time—just strength enough left to gather chips for fire.

"March 5—No rain till night. Caught 52 canaries. Lloyd was up six hours today. I got him some wood and four buckets of chips and some water.

"March 6—Rained all day lightly. Caught 38 canaries today. They are the only things that are keeping us alive. Lloyd is a lot worse today and my legs are badly swollen to the hips. If the ship don't come in by the 10th or 12th at the latest we are done for. Just salt left and four matches.

"March 7—Caught three canaries today, and one small trout. That's all we have had to eat. Rained all day, a fine rain. Lloyd is still in bed. His head is very bad. I am getting weaker daily. My knees are shaking now.

"March 8—Clear all day — caught 65 canaries. Tasted good after gaunt day. Neither one hardly had the strength to get them clean.

"March 9—Showering. Caught 41 canaries today. I had to crawl out for water today. No strength left to get wood. Burning moss off the bunk. Starvation is the most suffering on earth. Oh God, please send in a plane.

"Sunday, March 10—(Lloyd writing)I was in bed, Jim too tired to write.

156

"Monday—I was in bed. Jim, took sick in the stomach—canary bone.

"Tuesday—I was in bed. Nothing at all to eat. Jim still awfully sick.

"Wednesday—I was still in bed. Jim still sick. Caught a couple of canaries.

"Thursday—I was in bed. So was Jim.

"Friday—I got up for a while today. Crawled around and got a fire on. How, I don't know. Caught some canaries. Can't think straight enough to count them any more. Jim can hardly move and I can't help him. He has no power of his bowels at all. This is the worst hell either one of us has gone through. I don't know how much longer we can stick it. I got some rain water under the drip, so that will help. I'm sure God helped me get up today and gave me a little strength. I don't know many prayers but we both do nothing, day and night, but pray.

"Saturday, March 16—Jim worse today—nothing but skin and bone. I got some more canaries. I can hardly move around—so may the Lord have mercy on our souls. If we don't get out within a couple of days, dear mother, we have nobody else to blame but ourselves. But I've been praying always for you to send a plane in. We couldn't think of hiking when our grub got low, on account of floods, and there was one half dozen or more (prospectors) who said they would be in.... So this is what we get for taking chances.

"Sunday, March 17—Dear Mother: Jim died today at 2 p.m. This might be the last I'll have nerve to write, so if I do anything wrong please forgive me. I can't stick it any longer. The Bible is packed in the bottom of my packsack and I haven't the strength to get it out so I can't even say a decent prayer for poor old Jim."

After writing that last entry, Lloyd Coombs shot himself with his .30-30 rifle.

When we arrived at the cabin there were still dead birds on the floor, left uneaten when the two men became too weak to clean and eat them. Outside the door hung a pint bottle, sealed and suspended from a peg, half full of flesh taken from the birds and squirrels, put there "for a rainy day," and overlooked when they were unable to crawl from the cabin.

One aspect of the tragedy which puzzled veteran outdoorsmen was why the trappers did not hike out when they realized their food supply was inadequate. Zeballos was 25 miles away and Englewood about 40. Flood conditions were mentioned in the diary but this should have been no bar said woodsmen familiar with the rain-swept hinterland. Ryckman, in particular, was a veteran of many years in the woods, several in that locality, and Coombs was no tyro.

Dr. Jack Kelly, one of Zeballos' two physicians, said the men should have had no great difficulty in coming out, even though flood conditions were bad, unless an unrevealed incident had prevented them.

"The hike out is tough," he said, "but other chaps have done it. I can't understand why they didn't try it when they saw they were going to be short. I can't understand, either, where all their food went. It should have lasted them longer than that."

Why the trappers' food was gone months before they planned will remain a mystery. Was it because they had been unable to kill game to supplement the 1,500 pounds of supplies they took in with them?

Their puzzling decision to stay at the cabin rather than hike out was probably best explained by Constable Winegarden. He said he believed that they could have walked out easily in December or January before they lost their strength, instead of waiting for rescue by plane.

"Ryckman was an experienced woodsman and knew the country well," said Winegarden. "He knew the country well from many trips in to Vernon Lake. Game is scarce there, but there is lots of fish in the lake, and lots of elk and bear about five or 10 miles north. Ryckman knew this.

"They were not more than a week's hike from help. My theory is that their faith in rescue from the outside was their undoing. Even when they were running low on grub they continued to believe some pilot would happen in at Vernon Lake — and they held to this belief until they were too weak to trek out."

A selection of HERITAGE HOUSE titles

B.C. Provincial Police Stories

Volume 1 contains stories of true cases, reconstructed from police files and B.C. provincial archives by Deputy Commissioner **Cecil Clark**. Read about the man who was hanged by a thread, tragedy that stalked the Silver Trail, the men who were murdered by mistake, and fifteen others.

Volume 2 includes West Kootenay's tragic miner who died eight times, murder on Okanagan Lake, when Death rode a pinto pony, the cremation of Siboo Singh, Kitwancool drums that throbbed a war dance, the parking ticket that killed three men, and the hangman's tree at Lillooet.

Vol. 1 • ISBN 1-895811-77-5 • **128 pages** • **$9.95**
Vol. 2 • ISBN 1-895811-83-X • **128 pages** • **$9.95**

Outlaws & Lawmen of Western Canada

Volume 1 of this anthology depicts many of Western Canada's most dramatic crimes. Alberta's Swift Runner eats his family; Saskatchewan's first stage holdup; the 1880 death of Manitoba's police chief; B.C.'s Phantom of the Rangeland; and others. Includes about 80 photos.

More drama in Volume 2. In 1884, Jess Williams was the first man hanged in Calgary; Almighty Voice's murder of a policeman in 1895 caused six other deaths. Read of B.C.'s hanging that set a world record, the McLean Gang, Manitoba's first official outlaw, and many others. 80 photos and maps.

Volume 3 features B.C.'s murdering cannibal, the Mad Trapper of Rat River, Saskatchewan's midnight massacre, blazing guns at Banff, Yukon's Christmas Day assassins, stone-age murderers, Winnipeg's Prairie Strangler, and many others. 100 photos and maps.

Vol. 1 • ISBN 1-895811-79-1 • **128 pages** • **$10.95**
Vol. 2 • ISBN 1-895811-85-6 • **128 pages** • **$10.95**
Vol. 3 • ISBN 0-919214-88-6 • **160 pages** • **$11.95**

Totem Poles and Tea

As a nurse/teacher, **Hughina Harold** spent two years in a remote village in the 1930s and "witnessed things that should not be forgotten."

An engaging book that captures the mood of BC's west coast...it brings to mind an adult version of Anne of Green Gables...*a must read for anyone who considers himself or herself a BCer."*
Vancouver Sun.

ISBN 1-895811-11-2
• 192 pages • $17.95

Tales of a Pioneer Journalist

This anthology offers the finest work of one of B.C.'s great nineteenth-century newspapermen, **David Williams Higgins**, a former Speaker in the B.C. legislature.

ISBN 1-895811-24-4 • 192 pages • $16.95

White Slaves of the Nootka:

In 1803, the *Boston* was attacked by Nootka Indians off Vancouver Island and all but two of her 27-man crew were massacred. **John R. Jewitt** was kept as a slave for two years, facing death daily. This account, enhanced with photos, was first published in 1815, and 180 years later, remains one of the great stories of the nineteenth century.

ISBN 0-919214-51-7 • 128 pages • $9.95

Lost Bonanzas of Western Canada

Outlaw loot, lost mines, and sunken bullion. Are the treasues real or imaginary? **Garnet Basque** tells the stories, all of which have been checked for validity. Both books feature colour photos and maps.

Vol. 1 • ISBN 1-895811-40-6
• 160 pages • $14.95
Vol. 2 • ISBN 1-895811-86-4
• 144 pages • $14.95